CLARIFY

12 Principles to Illuminate Your Calling to the Marketplace

DENEEN TROUPE-BUITRAGO

HIGH BRIDGE BOOKS
HOUSTON

CLARIFY
by Deneen Troupe-Buitrago

Copyright © 2018 by Deneen Troupe-Buitrago
All rights reserved.

Printed in the United States of America
ISBN (Paperback): 978-1-946615-97-8
ISBN (eBook): 978-1-946615-13-8

High Bridge Books titles may be purchased in bulk for educational, business, fundraising, or sales promotional use. For information please contact High Bridge Books via www.HighBridgeBooks.com/contact.

Published in Houston, Texas by High Bridge Books

Contents

Acknowledgements

I want to thank a long-time accountability partner and friend, Shannon Spencer, for inspiring this book. We worked together for over a year encouraging one another and spurring one another on to greatness in our businesses. We also collaborated on many projects and this book would not have happened if we had not decided to do a seven-day challenge to show women how to connect their faith and business. Her ruthless critique tightened up my writing and allowed God to download exactly what He wanted said on these pages. Thank you, Shannon, for allowing God to use you to make me better.

I also want to thank my editor, Emily Gehman. Her way of taking what I really wanted to say and make it coherent for others is a true gift. She has blessed me with her enthusiasm for the book as we worked relentlessly to get it out quickly. She has shown me that God has a plan for me with a group of women I did not know I had something to say to. I thank God for her showing me how I can live out the title "Titus Woman."

I have to thank my friend Amber Kleindl for letting me buy her Starbucks® and reading through the first drafts to check for biblical accuracy. She didn't allow me to stray too far off the path into my imagination and create a world where I was talking for

God. She kept me grounded theologically and made me cut a lot of themes where I took too much liberty.

To my daughter, Ysavelle, my first editor (I made her read everything). I want to thank her for all the 'AHAs' she shared. This let me know I was on to something that could speak to women about their work. Her creativity and candor make the work more fulfilling.

I also need to thank my daughter, Paola. She is the one who I stopped often to give me feedback on issues ranging from word choice, fonts, and cover art. She was also my go-to person for brainstorming and critiques. Both of my girls inspire me to do better and be what God has called me to be.

I want to thank my husband for letting me take the time (and spend the money) to follow my passions. God is opening up doors for both of us to walk through and I am excited that this book has given us both opportunity to see God work.

A thank you page would not be complete without thanking Darren Shearer, the publisher. Thank you for believing in this project and in me as a writer.

Be filled to overflowing,
Deneen

Introduction

"How can I serve God more?"

This one deep question is what gave life to this book. I've been asked this question by businesswomen over and over again. And, it's a good question—one that deserves unique and specialized attention... one that we each need to answer as we live and move in our respective businesses.

How can we serve God more?

In exploring what God requires of each of us as women, I have been given insights into God's Word I've never thought about before. God has shown me that how I was taught to think about serving Him—and maybe how you were taught as well—was limiting. In this modern age, we may think the Bible is outdated and has nothing to say to us modern women. That is a lie Satan loves to use to keep us feeling trapped, guilty, and defeated.

The women in this book lived in different cultures and times in history, yet each one served God through her own unique gifts, talents, and personality. Each teaches an important principle for how we can show up in our world today, just as they showed up in theirs.

Open yourself to create the life of service God designed for you. Allow God to speak to your heart and whisper the path—the adventure—He has for you. God placed you in the marketplace for a reason. I want to release you from the guilt you may feel for not living up to a standard set by your family, your peers, or your faith community. Stop trying to do it all, and start doing what God planned for you to do.

The Great Commission tells us to "go and make disciples." Your "go" is right where you are in the workplace, and the disciples are those God has put in your sphere of influence.

The women in this book only did what was right in front of them. Likewise, God is calling you to look at what is right in front of you. Use the equipping, resources, and wisdom He gives you to impact those He has placed in your everyday life. God placed you in your marketplace to be His representative to the business world. You have a distinct role to play, and this book will help you find clarity for what God is calling you to do.

As you complete the exercises around each woman's principle and apply them to what God wants for your specific business—for your work—I pray you will shed the old mindset you may have and bust open the limits you have placed on serving God. God is inviting you to loosen the grip of man-made constraints on your life of service to Him. He wants you to walk in freedom, make decisions based on what He shows you, and live out your complete calling.

Paul's prayer to the Ephesians for their spiritual growth is my prayer for you, too. Only by nurturing the vertical relationship with God first can you have any success with the horizontal relationships in your life. Connecting faith and business begins with your faith. My prayer is that you will learn from the women in this book and be strengthened in your faith. I also pray you will be inspired by their stories and emboldened to live out your calling through your business. The following is Paul's prayer for you (as well as mine):

…I fall to my knees and pray to the Father, the Creator of everything in heaven and on earth. I pray that from his glorious, unlimited resources he will empower you with inner strength through his Spirit. Then Christ will make his home in your hearts as you trust in him. Your roots will grow down into God's love and keep you strong. And may you have the power to understand, as all God's people should, how wide, how long, how high, and how deep his love is. May you experience the love of Christ, though it is too great to understand fully. Then you will be made complete with all the fullness of life and power that comes from God. Now all glory to God, who is able, through his mighty power at work within us, to accomplish infinitely more than we might ask or think. Glory to him in the church and in Christ Jesus through all generations forever and ever! Amen. Ephesians 3:14b-21(NLT)

Be filled to overflowing,
Deneen

About This Book

Just like each of these biblical businesswomen had a unique relationship with God, He longs to have the same with you. With each woman you study, you'll see how her relationship with God informed her business and operations in distinct and amazing ways. And with each chapter, you'll have the opportunity to deepen your relationship with God and invite Him to partner with you in your business in new ways.

You'll see throughout each chapter Heart, Soul, Mind, and Strength activities designed to take you through each principle. They are in the form of reflection questions, prayer exercises, and spaces to think, plan, and write goals and actions steps for your business.

Heart Activities

As you read about these biblical businesswomen, use these reflection questions to explore how each woman can inform your business and relationships. Some of the questions will be easy to answer quickly, while others may take more thought time and perhaps even some journaling. Feel free to take as much time as you need for each question.

Soul Activities—Praying in Color

If you've spent any time in a traditional church setting, it's likely you know how to pray, but also know it can become boring or mundane. Of course, speaking to God, the Creator of the Universe, is anything but boring or mundane, but at times the traditional bow-your-head, close-your-eyes posture of prayer is inadequate for the words we're saying or the emotions we're feeling. Praying in Color is a way to express the things your heart longs to say to God in a little bit different format. It is neither better nor worse than "traditional" prayer; it's just different, and may provide a new and fresh way for you to relate to God.

The Praying in Color sections blend prayer and worship with coloring and doodling as a more tactile way to converse with God. You'll need some coloring utensils—colored pencils, markers, crayons, pens—whatever is your favorite to work with. Go pick out a journal you love that has no lines on the pages, or grab a stack of blank paper to use for each Praying in Color section. You'll use your creativity and your heart's thoughts to create beautiful pages of prayer. These times of creative worship can make your prayers come alive, vibrant with color, taking your prayers from black-and-white words to a range of hues and passions.

Each Praying in Color session will guide you to focus on a specific topic—like your favorite name or attribute of God—but you have creative control to design and build your prayer. Enjoy this innovative and expressive way to talk with God.

This technique is not unique to me. It was first introduced by Sybil MacBeth in her book, Praying in Color. This book transformed my prayer-life. I went from thinking of myself as a terrible pray-er to a prayer warrior. She has given me permission to use the technique and I have taken it beyond what she includes in her book.

Mind Activities

At the end of each section, you will have the opportunity to respond to the chapter's principle and create a goal for applying the principle to your own business. It may be a simple goal that can be completed quickly and become part of your business model right away. Or, it may be something larger that will be broken down and taken in steps.

Either way, you are in control of how you use what God is speaking to you about your business. He has a specific calling unique to you. Don't rush through these activities or think you must come up with the perfect plan right away. Work through the exercises and let God tell you what the goal should be for you.

Goals need to be SMART: Specific, Measurable, Attainable, Relevant, and Time-bound. A good goal includes all of these elements. Some of the goals you will be asked to write will be specific and include all of these elements. For other principles you will create an ongoing goal so the time-bound element may be modified. As you complete goals and grow in your business, new goals will emerge. Be sure to revisit the goal every eight to twelve weeks to check on your progress and adjust as necessary.

Each Mind Activity will have a prompt for you to think through your SMART goal. Use the space provided to record the parts before you write the goal.

Strength Activities

Without a concrete plan, your goal will not become a reality. These activities are designed as a tool to deconstruct the goal into a workable plan of action. You will have an opportunity to write out the how-it-will-happen part of the process. You will be guided step-by-step to help you be successful at implementing the goals God has for your business.

Guided Imagery Activities

Again, if you've spent time in traditional churches, guided imagery might be a new concept for you. But don't freak out—it's not heretical, and while it does employ controlled breathing and contemplation, it's not like Eastern meditation practices. Like the Praying in Color exercises, the guided imagery activities will provide a new and fresh way to think about your relationship with God and move closer to Him.

In the guided imagery activities, you'll be directed to lie down, close your eyes, and imagine a scene. One of the free resources you received with this book is a series of recordings for these activities (see resources page). I'll talk you through where you'll be and you'll think about what's surrounding you: the background noises, smells, textures, etc. The text of the recording is listed for you in each chapter. Read through the text first so you get an idea of what you'll be focusing on. Then prepare yourself with these breathing patterns (you'll do this for each guided imagery exercise):

First, create an environment where you can be completely relaxed and undistracted as you move through the guided imagery activity. Light a candle or turn on your diffuser to set a mellow mood.

Lie on the floor, your yoga mat, or on your bed. Place one hand on your chest and the other on your belly. Take a deep breath in through your nose, ensuring the diaphragm (not the chest) inflates with enough air to create a stretch in the lungs. You should be able to feel that stretch.

Begin breathing in a 12-second cycle: Breathe in for four counts, hold it for four counts, and then exhale for four counts. Repeat this six to ten times, or for two minutes.

After you've relaxed with the breathing, continue to breathe slowly as you imagine the scene. As you listen to the recording, I'll guide you to picture yourself in a setting similar to that biblical businesswoman's, and you'll see how each story can deepen your relationship with God.

After you complete each Guided Imagery activity, lie there for as long as you wish until you are ready to move. Continue breathing deeply until you want to get up and reflect on the activity. Use your journal or a piece of paper to reflect on what God revealed to you through the activity. Be sure to record the feelings and thoughts you experienced as you spent time with God in this unique way.

Are You Ready?

Now that you know how to use the elements in this book, are you ready to CLARIFY your calling in the marketplace? Let's take a look at these eleven women and see what they have to say about connecting faith and business. And in the process, you'll see your vision and God's equipping come together for maximum impact in your marketplace. Let's go!

1

Eve:
Her Work Was Good

Read the biblical account of Eve in Genesis 1 and 2.

Principle: **God has a plan for my business.**

God Designed You to Work, and He Called it Good

We begin with Eve not just because she is the first woman in the Bible, but because in her creation, we see how God established work for each of us. Genesis 1:27 tells us God created man in his own image and that He created them male and female. And then in chapter two, Eve's story unfolds, showing how and why she was created: She was created to be an ezer—a helper. The only other person given this designation in Scripture is God (Psalm 30:10; 54:4). Imagine being able to put that on your résumé!

As an ezer, Eve is also designed to work alongside Adam in the physical work of caring for the garden. They're instructed to be fruitful and multiply, as well as subdue and govern it. These are both physical and intellectual tasks, neither of which God distinguishes as more important. There is no mention about which type of work is more significant or more godly. All work is necessary and, as God calls it, Good.

Have you ever stopped to think about your work being Good? I love looking at my work this way. As an entrepreneur and businesswoman, I know we can get tied up in our everyday routine and sometimes miss the Good in our work. Think about it this way: God planted this seed of thought in your brain about starting your business. His creativity worked through you, as His image bearer, to bring about the work you are doing.

God is so creative! Imagine creating all the colors, textures, and fragrances in the world. Each tree, flower, animal, rock formation, water source and cloud scream His creativity. You get to reflect that creativity by being the unique person He created you to be! Your work is all God's plan. What He set in motion from the foundation of the world—work—is now His perfect plan for you and your business. And it is Good.

God gave Eve work to fulfill His creation. He expects you to continue the work, producing and fulfilling your unique contribution. Your work may look different in the various seasons of your life, but only you can fulfill the plan God has for you.

And God gives us exactly what we need to be creative! This is how you can reflect His glory through work. He intended work to have meaning (Genesis 2:15). It is not done alone, but in relationship with God and others (Genesis 1:26, 27; 2:18). And it grows to be fruitful (Genesis 1:28). Work also shows God's provision (Genesis 1:29-30; 2:8-14), designed with limits so we depend on Him (Genesis 2:3, 17).

This is the beauty of being in relationship with God—His plans are always Good and perfect. Because Jesus came and gave each of us new life, we belong to God (1 Corinthians 6:19-20). Your business may be Good; God wants to make it better. This takes cooperation with Him as you think and ask Him to align your goals with His for your business. Then your work becomes much more: It takes on new life and transforms into worship (Romans 12:1).

How have you been looking at your business? Is it a means to make money? A passion you are pursuing? Something you inherited? Is it a stepping stone to the next thing? God has you in this place right now for His purpose. You are the only you that will ever exist. And you exist now to fulfill His work in your life through your business.

Just as Eve was created for the work God gave her, He has given you unique work, too. He has a plan for your business, and it is Good.

Heart Activity

Reflection Questions:

What is Good about your work?

How do you think God is involved in your work?

After reading this section, what has changed in your thinking about work?

How will you cooperate with God to align your goals with His?

Prayer

Father, thank You for Eve's story. Thank you for creating us for community with You and with each other. I'm thankful I am not alone in creating the life and work You designed for me. Thank

You for showing me You created my work specifically for me and You equip me to do it. I understand the ideas You have already given me are just the start of what You have planned for me. I want to partner with You in my business; I invite You in. It is all for You. I know Your plan is exactly right for me and I trust You. In Jesus' name, amen.

God Designed Your Work, and He Calls it Good

Being the first woman to exist puts Eve in a very special situation. She was the first to do everything! She was the first wife, the first homemaker, the first mom, and with Adam, the first keeper of a garden and first worshipper of God. She didn't have a mentor to learn from, a mother or grandmother to get advice from, and she only had her husband for friendship—and he was new to all this, too.

What she did have was a dependence on God. She enjoyed God's company in the Garden, His care and protection, and His friendship. She and Adam grew in relationship with each other and with God (Genesis 2:22-24).

Adam and Eve grew together through their work. We are designed this way by God; we bond with our coworkers as we accomplish a common goal. I'm sure you have experienced this before. Coworkers are essential to your success in the marketplace. The very word coworker comes from the words helper and partner. Who are the people in your day-to-day you are coworking with for your success?

Eve's coworker was her husband. I can imagine them together at the end of the day discussing the day's work. It is an intimate setting as they sit in a clearing, maybe with a warm fire going. God was there, too; they expected Him in the cool of the evening (Genesis 3:8). I see her beaming with joy as they shared their day with God and He commends her work. I see them planning the next day as they continued the work God had given them.

This gathering was probably her favorite time of the day. I know it would be for me—meeting with God to tell Him about my day and Him helping me plan the next. Amazing.

I'm sure there were days Eve felt a real learning curve—just like we experience—but I know God must have been the best consoler and motivator. God allows these days so we learn and grow through our work. His goal for us is to learn dependence on Him in a very tangible way.

Your work is to do God's work; we have already established that. He can redeem your work to glorify Him, but what He really wants is to redeem you. Placing God first in your thoughts, your day, your plans, your everything, puts you in the right place to understand God is your helper (ezer), your partner, and your coworker in your business.

God wants to be in your work; He created it for you to do. He's waiting for you to make Him the center of your business and your life. God has a plan for your business, and it is Good.

Soul Activity

Take some time to sit in the garden with God for some Praying in Color. In your journal or on a piece of paper, write in the center of your page the name for God you most love. Some ideas are: Savior, Counselor, Holy One, Redeemer, Healer, Friend, etc. Other words may be more of a feeling: Love, Honor, Glory, Worthy. Usually it's easy to find your word by completing the phrase, "God, You are..."

Draw a bubble, cloud, or shape around the name you chose or just start doodling. The drawing becomes your prayer space, a kind of small prayer closet.

As you add color, lines, marks, and shapes, focus on the name you chose. Ask God to be part of your prayer time with or without words. If words come, pray them, incorporate them into your page; if no words come, enjoy the silence and keep coloring.

Worship God here, using color and/or words to focus only on Him.

Then, invite God into your business. Invite Him to shape your goals and plans. Surrender your work to Him. It is Good.

Prayer

Thank You, Lord, for this time to come before You and worship. Thank You for the time I can take out of my busy day to focus on You. I do invite you into my business, my plans, and my goals. Thank You for caring enough for me to want to partner with me. Help me recognize You are with me and speaking to me every day, and help me to listen. In Jesus' name, amen.

Eve Guided Imagery

This is a guided imagery exercise. Read it through completely before you begin the activity. Refer to the instructions for creating your environment and the breathing exercise in the front of this book to begin relaxing.

After you have relaxed with the breathing, continue to breathe slowly and imagine this scene:

Go to the garden again. Imagine a lush area of vegetation. There are large trees and dense bushes everywhere. Look around and see yourself in the middle of this paradise.

Focus ahead and see there is a path through the growth. Begin to walk through the trees. Up ahead you see a patch of sunlight where the trees have opened. As you walk, listen to the bugs buzzing and the birds calling. Breathe in the sweet smells from the flowers growing nearby. Feel the soft breeze as it comes across your face.

Walk into the sunlight, the garden clearing, and become aware of God's presence. He is there waiting for you, just like He would have been for Eve. Imagine God as light and warmth entering your body. Allow it to fill you up with each breath.

Imagine sitting down with God and talking about your day. Tell Him what you have been doing. Tell Him about your business. Tell Him how much you love Him. Now listen. What does God tell you about His plan for you? How does He want your work to glorify Him? What is He telling your heart?

Lay down in the grass and allow God's presence to fill you up again. Feel the warmth of the sun in the clearing. Close your eyes and thank God for His time with you. Thank Him for meeting with you and speaking to your heart.

Lay there as long as you wish until you are ready to move. Continue breathing deeply until you want to get up and reflect.

Response Activity

Once you have completed the imagery exercise, use your journal or a piece of paper to reflect on what God revealed to you about His plan for you. Be sure to record the feelings and thoughts you experienced as you went to the garden to meet with God.

Prayer

Lord, You are amazing! Thank You for who You are. I love You, Lord, and thank You for revealing so much to me about my business. Let me find time each day to sit in the garden with You. Help me make You a priority as we partner together in life and business. I know You have a plan for my business and it is Good. In Jesus' name, amen.

Mind Activity

Principle: **God has a plan for my business.**

Eve enjoyed God's company in the Garden of Eden. She enjoyed His care and protection. She and Adam grew in relationship with each other and with God (Genesis 2:22-24).

How can you cooperate with God so you align your goals with His plan for your work? This activity is designed to help you create a goal to live out Eve's Principle. Goals need to be SMART: Specific, Measurable, Attainable, Relevant, Time-bound. Since this goal is ongoing, it may change and look different as you grow.

I want to give you an example of my goal for this principle to get you started. My goal for understanding my work is Good is this: "I will recognize God as my Boss and will meet with Him each day by making an appointment in my calendar. I will use my journal to allow God to impress on me where He wants me to go and record it. I will ask God to take things out of my life and off my plate. I will accept His will for me and not run after the things I think I need. I want to cooperate with God for my Good."

Specific: Recognizing God as my Boss
Measurable: Recording thoughts each day
Attainable: Putting the appointment in my calendar
Relevant: Cooperating with God makes my business
    Good
Time-bound: Daily

God gave you this vision along with your specific set of skills, talents, gifts, and experiences to bring your uniqueness into the world. No one just like you has ever existed, and God has given you a purpose, a job only you can accomplish. Follow your God-given vision. It is Good.

Write out your Goal.

S
M
A
R
T

Strength Activity

Principle: **God has a plan for my business.**

Creating a goal is great! Having an action plan is better. Deconstructing your goal into bite-sized, actionable steps is next. These steps are habits you create to live out the principle in your business.

If you have written your goal with the SMART format, this should be an easy activity. I also know having an example helps you get started.

Goal: Meet with God each day

- Decide how much time each day.
- Put appointment in planner.
- Set alarm or create another reminder.
- When reminder happens, have the appointment (do the behavior).
- Record thoughts, prayers, and impressions in journal.

Now it's your turn to create an action plan for your goal.

Prayer

God, You are in all I do. Thank You for giving me the business vision and I pray to do Your will in all areas of my life. Help me create the goals and actions steps that will move me forward in Your calling on my life. In Jesus' name, amen.

2

Esther:
Royal Responsibility

Read the biblical account of Esther in the book named for her.

Principle: **I am called to the marketplace.**

Accepting Your Role

Esther's story is one many of us—even you—can relate to. I bet you didn't expect to hear that! If you know anything about Esther, you probably think of her as the brave queen who saved her people…and you think, That is not me. Let's look at the beginning of the story though, the part where you may see yourself.

Esther is a Jewish woman living in exile in Persia. The Persians have taken the Jewish people as their own and the nation of Israel is no longer self-governed. She is probably the third or fourth generation to live there. Persia is all she knows, but she is well-versed in Jewish history and tradition, thanks to Moredecai, the man who raised her. She's an orphan, and she's described as being obedient to him as her cousin-turned-adopted father (Esther 2:10). I imagine she has some abandonment issues, has developed a tough outer persona, and has learned some street smarts. I see Esther as a survivor, doing all she can to blend in with her surroundings. For one, she has changed her name (Esther 2:7). I am sure her Farsi—the language of the Medes and Persians—is as flawless as her Hebrew. And her style and hair are right on trend.

We hide in our culture, too. We blend in, especially at work or in business. We want everyone to see our expertise and experience so we can move up the proverbial ladder. We may be guilty of compromising our morals to go along with accepted practices and work for our own interests. Are you hiding your true self at work each day?

Esther can't hide; she is beautiful. When she goes to get water, heads turn. I wouldn't be surprised if the boys aren't the only ones looking at her; the girls are straining to see what Esther is wearing so they can copy. Beauty may be skin deep, but we soon learn Esther has brains to accompany her beauty.

So, when Queen Vashti is banished from the king's sight, he begins the search for a new queen. Hundreds of girls are rounded up so the king has the very best to choose from. Imagine that interview: "Spend the night with me," the king says, "and if I like you better than the others, you will have the position."

Esther is taken to the palace, where she must "endure" twelve months of beauty treatments! Day in and day out of oils, perfumes, facials, and massages. It sounds like it could be heaven. But then I think of the waxing, diet, and fitness that probably went along with it; that could be brutal. Esther was surviving the best she could, using the resources available to her. But God was placing her in position.

Esther is cooperative and charming, and wins the admiration of Hegai, the attendant in charge of the candidates. Esther uses her wit and cleverness, but it was really God's hand that gave her favor (Esther 2:9). I'm sure her survival instincts were looking for opportunities to make the best out of this appalling situation. She was trying to actually thrive in an environment hostile toward her faith in God.

This hostile environment, in many ways, exists for you, too. I'm sure you have been in situations you found appalling and had to survive. Maybe it was tolerating the difficult coworker on an important project. It could be dealing with a boss or business partner who demeans you. Or even an embezzlement situation that left you picking up the pieces.

And Esther? She is still hiding who she really is. In fact, Mordecai comes every day to check on her and urges her not to tell anyone of her heritage. The text doesn't say, but I think Mordecai sees God working in ways he couldn't yet identify. Both of them played it so cool.

At last, the "interview." She follows Hegai's advice and enters the King's chambers prepared with the essentials to win his heart. And of course, she does. She becomes queen and accepts her role in the palace.

Smart Esther plays the game correctly to get the prize. She was hiding her true identity, but God was giving her opportunity for greatness. He was calling her to the political workplace of the palace by orchestrating everything in her favor.

You, too, must accept your role as royalty in your marketplace.

Heart Activity

Reflection Questions:

What are the gifts, talents, and skills that move you forward in your business?

How do you identify with Esther in your own marketplace?

Describe a time when you saw God's favor in something you have done in your business.

What could God be placing you into position for in the marketplace?

Prayer

Thank You, Lord, for my business. I know You have placed me in the marketplace so I can use the talents, gifts, and abilities You have given me. I thank You for guiding me in ways I don't understand at times; I trust You to work through me even in the most difficult situations. I know You are working everything in my favor and for Your glory. I praise You for who You are. I thank You for coming into my life. Transform me into Your image more and more each day. In Jesus' name, amen.

Acting In Your Role

We pick up the story of Esther four years or so after she has become Queen. We do not know what she has been through in these years, the ups and downs of palace life, if she has children or not. We're not told if she is even still the king's favorite. Her life may not have been exactly what she thought it would be as Queen, but she has an inner strength that keeps her going.

And like Esther, our lives are imperfect and not always what we expect. We need God's grace. We divide our world and sometimes forget our identity, whose we really are. But God has made us royal priests and kings—queens!—for His work (I Peter 2:9).

Your identity doesn't depend on who you are or what you do for a living. It depends on who God is and what He has done for you.

But now, Esther's life comes to a crisis point. Haman, a man who hates Mordecai, has risen to power and threatens the lives of all the Jewish people. Mordecai's response of mourning catches Esther's attention and they have a conversation. Esther is left to decide her next step. She cannot hide who she is any longer; she knows that won't keep her safe. She has been positioned as Queen to actually do something, to fulfill her destiny.

As a believer in Jesus, you, too, have your position—your business—in order to do something. God calls us living stones He is building to offer spiritual sacrifices pleasing to Him (1 Peter 2:5). We are chosen as royal priests to show others the goodness of God (1 Peter 2:9).

Living out this royal priesthood in the marketplace requires sacrifice. Esther shows her sacrifice, risking her safety for a chance to speak with the king (Esther 4:11). What kind of sacrifices might you make in your business to demonstrate you are a royal priest? It could be forgiving the debt of a client or forgiving someone who has betrayed your trust. It may be giving more of your earnings to God's work. Or sacrificing time in your business to make your family a priority. These are all pleasing to God.

Now this is the part of the story I love. Esther knows in order to have any chance of saving her people, she must be prepared. So, she calls her team to fast and pray with her. In fact, she calls for the entire Jewish population to pray with her! She knows God has called her to do something and realizes her need for Him to help her accomplish the task. You can feel the shift in her purpose and motivation for being in the palace.

We must make this same type of shift—to understand our purpose and motivation for doing business is to demonstrate God's love by making Him known to others.

God rewards Esther's sacrifice by granting her access to the king in order to proclaim her identity, the second responsibility of a royal priest. Again God uses Esther's intelligence to orchestrate the best outcome. By the time she is ready to reveal her identity and her request (to spare the Jewish nation), the king's heart has been softened by God to receive it positively (Esther 7:5).

Esther was no longer hiding. She had her intelligence, resources, beauty, and charm that put her right where God wanted and needed her to be. You have your talents, skills, gifts, and abilities that put you where God wants and needs you to be. Your workplace, your colleagues, your business partners, your vendors, your employees—your sphere of influence is where you are called to be God's light. God does not want you to hide anymore!

As a believer in Jesus, you are called to reign in life (Romans 5:17). Your other claim to royalty is as a queen for His Kingdom. And just as you have duties as a royal priest, there are attributes you can display as Christ's queen in your marketplace. Esther demonstrates the power of royalty by providing an opportunity to save her people. You can provide for others, too, by sharing your spiritual gifts (teaching, discernment, administration to name a few): by adding economic value and giving to others to meet a need; by creating economic opportunities for others though employment, collaboration, and sales; by showing mercy and providing relief to those hurting financially, whether a client or employee.

And your last responsibility as royalty, a queen, in the marketplace is protecting those in your sphere of influence. Esther protected her people by acting when the time was critical so the Jews wouldn't be destroyed. You can protect your own by making wise and righteous decisions that do good, by voicing encouragement, support, and positive words to those around you, and by praying for those you connect with in your business.

You will always live in accordance with your understanding of who you are. More importantly, you must understand WHOSE you are. Believe you are called to the business you are in right now. Believe what the Bible says: you are a royal priest called to offer spiritual sacrifices to God and to proclaim Him to your coworkers, clients, vendors, bosses, board members, and any other person in the marketplace (1 Peter 3:15). And as a queen, you are called to provide for and protect those within your sphere of influence in business. You are on the frontline each and every day. Wear your crown with the same attitude as Christ (Philippians 2:5) by being a servant who reflects the goodness of the Father.

Soul Activity

God says we can come before Him in His throne room and ask Him anything (Revelation 8:3-4). Today you will be Praying in Color about God's call for you as a royal priest and queen. In the top half of your page write Royal Priest and in the bottom half of your page write Queen.

Draw a bubble, cloud, or shape around each word. Focus on one concept at a time as you color and doodle on the page. The drawing becomes your prayer being lifted to the Father, up to God's throne.

Add color, lines, marks and shapes. Ask God to reveal to you how you can serve others through your business by sacrificing, proclaiming Him, providing for and protecting those in your sphere of influence. Draw the images and write the words He impresses on your heart.

Pray this prayer often as you seek to follow God's call for you in the marketplace.

Prayer

God, You are amazing. I am in awe of what You have called me to be as Your follower. I am honored to be called a royal priest and queen in the marketplace. I pray for Your guidance each day, as I live out this calling, by offering spiritual sacrifices pleasing to You. I pray for the courage to proclaim whose I am to those in my sphere of influence, and I accept my responsibility to them to provide for and protect them. I do all this for You, Lord. Create the shift in my perspective to see Your work done through me and give me the courage to do it. In Jesus' name, amen.

Esther Guided Imagery

This is a guided imagery exercise. Read it through completely before you begin the activity. Refer to the instructions for creating your environment and the breathing exercise in the front of this book to begin relaxing.

After you have relaxed with the breathing, continue to breathe slowly and imagine this scene:

You are standing at the entrance of a grand, open-aired room. Look around. Drink in the colors of the tiles inlaid on the floor and embedded in the walls. Let your eyes rise, following the marble columns that seem to reach to the sky. Notice how light filters through the sheer fabrics draped between the columns.

Step into the room and feel the cool tiles on your bare feet. The air is warm; the breeze light and refreshing. This is your coronation day. You will be crowned as a royal priest and queen for God's service. Excitement ripples through your stomach as you look toward the throne.

Yes, this is the throne room. The chair is large and made of gold. The jewels adorning it sparkle when the sunlight hits them. A brocade cushion with tassels covers the seat. It is magnificent.

God enters the room from the other side of the throne. He is holding a crown—your crown. It looks tiny in His powerful hands. He calls you closer to Him. You walk across the room so lightly it's as if you are floating.

As you stand before God, He lifts the crown so you can see the beautiful stones encircling it. He says you are chosen, a royal priest, holy, and that you belong to Him. And as a result, you can show others His goodness because He has called you.

You bow to your knees before Him and He places the crown on your head. You feel the weight of it rest on your head and know you are loved by the Father. Look up at Him and thank Him for who He is and what He has done for you. Thank Him for giving you such an honored commission for your life.

Stand and walk to your throne. Sit on the soft cushion and enjoy the moment. Close your eyes, push away your doubts, and rest in the fact that God will help you with your royal assignment.

Lie there as long as you wish until you are ready to move. Continue breathing deeply until you want to get up and reflect.

Response Activity

Once you have completed the guided imagery exercise, use your journal or a piece of paper to reflect on what God revealed to you about what it means to be His royal priest and queen. Be sure to record the feelings and thoughts you experienced as God crowned you for His service.

Prayer

Lord, this has been another amazing time learning about You! Thank You for who You are. I love You, Lord, and thank You for revealing who I am in You as a royal priest and queen. Let me find time each day to reflect on what You have called me to do in the marketplace. Help me rest in the fact that You have given me all the tools I need to show others Your goodness. Help me depend on You for strength to act on this knowledge; I know You have called me to the marketplace. In Jesus' name, amen.

Mind Activity

Principle: **I am called to the marketplace.**

We have all heard about comparison, the ugly thief of joy. It is easy to see someone else's success and think we cannot measure up. God has made you so different from others and you must begin to embrace this truth. He has called you to the marketplace for His specific purpose. No one else has your set of credentials to do the job He has called you to do. Only you show up as you. I love that.

I imagine Esther didn't feel she would make a difference with what she had to offer, beauty and charm. But GOD.

As royalty, you are called to offer spiritual sacrifices to God and to proclaim Him to your co-workers, clients, vendors, bosses, board members, etc. (1 Peter 3:15). As a queen, you are called to provide for and protect those within your sphere of influence.

For your goal, write out one way in each area you can begin (or continue) to live out these callings as queen.

Sacrifice

Proclaim

Provide for

Protect

Let me share with you how I answered these four areas in my business:

Sacrifice: Forgiven a payment someone owed me who had signed a contract.

Proclaim: Conduct my business honestly and with transparency as a believer in Jesus.

Provide for: Give service and value to my clients above what I have promised.

Protect: Praying for those I lead.

Create a SMART Goal that incorporates these four areas as a guide.

Here is an example: As a leader, I will always strive to show up with excellent service that goes beyond my clients' expectations by always acting with honesty and transparency to deliver tools they can use to grow in business. I will do this by praying for their needs, asking God to reveal to me how I can best serve them so they can succeed.

Write out your Goal.

S

M

A

R

T

Strength Activity

Principle: **I am called to the marketplace.**

Writing down your goal is one part of the equation. In fact, you are 80% more likely to complete a goal if you write it down. Now it is time to deconstruct it into actual items you can and will do next. Your SMART Goal is general, based on all four areas of your Royal Responsibility. Choose only one area you can concentrate on and create a plan that will help you demonstrate that quality (sacrifice, proclaim, provide, protect) to others and show Christ. Add the other areas until you have an action plan in place for each.

Make it something small, just a bite-sized activity you CAN (and will) do daily.

My Protect action plan includes a daily prayer time for those in my Networking Group. I write down their names and lift them up to the Father. I also tell them I pray for them and I ask for prayer requests via our secret Facebook group and at our meetings.

Write down your first area and the action you will do:

Prayer

God, You have given me the privilege of being a priest and queen in the marketplace. Thank You for this awesome opportunity to make You known through my business. I love that You have given me the exact abilities I need to show up in my business in the ways You want. I pray for opportunities to show You in these four areas of my business. Help me sacrifice and provide for my business partners, employees, clients, and customers. Teach me to protect my sphere of influence and protect those I lead as I proclaim You. In Jesus' name, amen.

3

Martha:
Connecting Faith &
Business

Read the Biblical account of Martha in Luke 10:38-42 and John 11:1-12:3.

Principle: **I give God glory through my business.**

Viewing Your Work Through Your Eyes

Martha is the woman I can most relate to in the Bible. Maybe you can, too. Workaholic—no, more like multitaskaholic—looking for significance, and feeling like you are doing it all alone. Martha is a leader, not a follower. She's the one who makes things happen. Martha's story is similar to many of ours as women: mothers, daughters, business owners, caregivers, carpoolers, party-planners. You get the picture.

We meet Martha doing what she loves: entertaining. Jesus and his disciples (more than the Twelve, I imagine) are in Bethany, Martha's town. She invites them to her home. You may know the story of Martha fussing around the kitchen to make and serve the perfect meal to honor Jesus, while her sister, Mary, sits at Jesus' feet.

The Bible does not go into detail about how many times Jesus has stopped at Martha's home during His three years of ministry, but I would have to imagine it was more often than we know. How else could she feel comfortable enough with Him to stop the action in the living room and complain about her sister's lack of help in front of everyone?

And even though Jesus scolds her, telling her Mary "has chosen the better part" (Luke 10:42), we never see Him say, "yes, you must be just like your sister and do what she is doing." I love that about Jesus. He never asks us to change our personalities or be someone we are not. He never tells her to stop working.

In fact, Martha is consumed with work. If we could give her some advice it might be to "work smarter, not harder," "delegate," "learn to say NO," and "take a spa day." Has anyone ever said something like that to you? It's not a problem with work; it is Martha's view of work that has gotten her into trouble.

First off, she has Jesus in her living room and she's worried about being the perfect hostess. Instead of being present and mindful in the moment she has been given and connecting with Jesus, she tries to earn her way into Jesus' heart (through His stomach). By doing things for Him, she believes it will bring her closer to Him. But her work is cutting her off from the one relationship she wants most. She is working so hard to impress Him she misses what is important—Him! The Bible says it's only by grace we come to the Father; faith is the only thing that saves us, and there is nothing we can do ourselves (Ephesians 2:8-9). Relationship is God's gift to us, and our work is our gift back to Him.

Martha's overwhelm comes from trying to do it all alone. She has the right idea bringing it to the attention of Jesus, but she doesn't get the answer she expected. Instead, she gets a wake-up call. We all have many responsibilities and, at times, not enough hours in the day. We have our Martha-like meltdowns. But God never intends for you to carry everything without Him. In fact, He promises rest for your soul (Matthew 11:28-29).

Martha is learning, though. By being in relationship with Jesus, she can't help but change from the inside out. Her personality is still bold; she is still organizing events and running her household. But she has been touched by Jesus. She has been given a new way to see her work.

Heart Activity

Reflection Questions:

In what ways do you relate to Martha?

Describe a time when have you been distracted by work or responsibilities and have missed the moment in front of you.

How is God changing your view of your work?

Prayer

Father, thank You for Your love and patience. You show me each day more and more of who You are. Help me take time to be with You. Help me prioritize my work so I don't miss You. You promise to give me rest if I come to You with everything. I never have to be alone with You as my partner. Help me rely on You for my strength each day as I give You glory with my business. In Jesus' name, amen.

Viewing Your Work Through God's Eyes

We get one last glimpse into Martha's story when her brother, Lazarus, has fallen ill and she sends for Jesus. (She is keeping close tabs on him and knows where he is.) But Jesus arrives too late and Lazarus dies. Again, Martha is entertaining important townspeople, working hard to serve those who have come to pay their respects. But when she hears that Jesus is coming down the road, she runs to meet him. She is no longer fussing over the work that must be done; she knows "this is the better" and goes to Jesus.

The mourners watch her rush past them, leaving the gathering. Does this mean she has abandoned her work? Because she is in relationship with Jesus, must she drop the work and ONLY be with Him? Does it mean we must choose between serving God and doing our work? Martha's story shows us there is no difference between the sacred and the secular. She leads her household and takes on all her responsibilities. Jesus never tells her to give all that up to follow Him. He wants her heart, but never tells her to separate her work-life from her faith-life. Her work serves the kingdom and is God-given. Her work is necessary in order to fulfill God's plan for her and bring Him glory. He wants her work to have purpose and meaning.

He wants that for you, too.

As we plan each day's activities we must focus on three key ideas: required, return, reward. What is required of me today? What activities give a return on my investment? (This might not always be financial.) And what is the reward for being involved in what I am doing? Seeing the activities of your entire life—specifically your work—as a means to give God glory is the starting point.

Martha is given a great honor on the road that day. She is credited as being the only person, other than Peter, to declare that

Jesus is "the Messiah, the Son of God" (John 11:27). How extraordinary for her to have been given such a measure of faith!

Martha continues to run her household and work. In the beginning, she may have thought she was just serving the Teacher, but it turned into an encounter that transformed her into a true disciple. She may have had to learn the hard way, but now she knows when it is important to work and when it is important to be with Jesus.

The last thing we see her doing in Scripture is working (John 12:2). She is serving Jesus. Just the place she wants to be. She is working and proclaiming her faith through it.

Martha has become the woman God intended her to be, and He's shown Martha how her work can glorify Him. She's still working, but now she's giving her heart to Jesus, not just her physical work.

Soul Activity

Martha learned that her faith-life and her work-life were intertwined. She could do her work and show God's glory through it. He has placed you in the marketplace to do the same thing. Today you will be Praying in Color about connecting your faith and business so you can show God's goodness and give Him glory. On your journal page or piece of paper, write the words Faith and Business side by side (you may want to turn the page in the landscape direction).

Begin to draw a bubble, cloud, or shape around each word and then connect the two words in some way using lines, drawings, and colors. Think about all the ways you can connect these two parts of your life. Ask God to show you how your work serves His kingdom. Ask God to use your business for His glory. Color and doodle on the page. Ask God to show you specific ways you can bring Him glory through your business. Thank Him for having purpose and meaning in your work.

Add colors, lines, marks and shapes. Ask God for wisdom to keep your work in its proper perspective. Draw the images and/or write the words He impresses on your heart as He reveals your calling in the marketplace.

Prayer

Father, thank You for the example of Martha. I love how You can take an overworked, responsible go-getter and create in her a heart for You. It has helped me realize You don't separate my faith-life from my work-life. You have given me my work for Your glory. Thank You, Lord, for creating me unique and that You have specific purpose and meaning for the work You have called me to. Help me glorify You in all I do. In Jesus' name, amen.

Martha Guided Imagery

This is a guided imagery exercise. Read it through completely before you begin the activity. Refer to the instructions for creating your environment and the breathing exercise in the front of this book to begin relaxing.

After you have relaxed with the breathing, continue to breathe slowly and imagine this scene:

You're standing on a tree-lined dirt road, flat and straight. You can see down the road a long way, and you can barely make out a figure coming toward you.

You feel the warmth of the day and hear the songs of all the different birds in the trees. You begin walking faster. As you get closer, you realize the figure is someone familiar. Your heart beats inside your chest with anticipation. You squint your eyes against the sunlight as it breaks through the trees so you can get a better look. Your feet seem to be moving even faster, and finally you recognize it is Jesus. And He's coming to meet you!

You take off running toward Him and you can see a smile—a big one—on His face. He holds out His arms ready to receive you. When you reach Him, you are laughing, breathless, and happy. You hug Him and He hugs you back. His arms feel strong and comforting around your back. He holds on until you let go.

Your breathing returns to normal. Tell Him how happy you are to have this time with Him. Thank Him for all the things He has taught you about connecting your faith and business. What does He say to you?

As you walk together, you hear the crunch of the pebbles under your feet and feel His strength next to you. Enjoy Jesus' company and listen to His words of encouragement and support. What is He saying to your heart? You walk together until you are at the place you began; it's time for you to return to your work.

Thank Him for meeting with you. Tell Him you will return often to learn more from Him. He reaches His hand out and touches your cheek; His kind eyes say how proud He is of you. You feel His love fill your entire being. You are happy.

Lie there as long as you wish until you are ready to move. Continue breathing deeply until you want to get up and reflect.

Response Activity

Once you have completed the imagery exercise, use your journal or a piece of paper to reflect on what God revealed to you about connecting your faith and business. What is it like to spend time with Him? Be sure to record the feelings and thoughts you experienced as you met Jesus on the road.

Prayer

God, thank You for what You have spoken to my heart today. Remind me to meet with You each day. As I connect my faith and business, help me see the God-moments when they happen. I pray to grow in my relationship with You. I pray to grow my business so I can give You glory. Father, help me be the woman You have called me to be. Help me show You in my marketplace. In Jesus' name, amen.

Mind Activity

Principle: **I give God glory through my business.**

Martha learned that her faith-life and her work-life were intertwined. She could do her work and show God's glory through it. He has placed you in the marketplace to do this also.

How has viewing your work through this lens given you a new perspective to your work? One thing that changed for me was how I viewed the money I made through work. I used to think I had a job so I could make money and do things for the ministry. Now I see money as a way I can be generous through my business. That's one way I give God glory through my work.

The goal for this principle is to see your work as a way you glorify God. Take some time to listen to God as He speaks to you about where you can start. Ask Him to reveal the areas where you are separating what you think is business (secular) from your faith (sacred).

Write out your Goal.

S

M

A

R

T

This is another goal that can be created as something you incorporate and do all the time in your business, or it can be something specific to what you need to think about right now. These goals are not static; they are meant to be re-evaluated and tweaked periodically.

Here is an example of one of my ongoing goals: When I present my 60-second commercial at networking events, I will include a line about connecting faith and business and tell others I am a faith-based/Christian entrepreneur.

Strength Activity

Principle: **I give God glory through my business.**

In reality, we are to give God glory in all that we do (1 Corinthians 10:31). For this reason, I want you to think through not only the business goal you have decided to write but also all the other parts of your life.

A good way to evaluate your activities is to see where they fall in the required-return-reward tool. Take a look at your daily schedule over the course of one week. List out the activities into the three areas: required, return, reward.

Write out the activities that are required first. This may include household responsibilities and work commitments.

Next, place the activities that have a good return on investment onto the second list. This may include making appointments for your business or building a relationship. It can also mean taking on new clients to make money.

Lastly, place the activities that bring you joy and contentment onto the last list. These are activities that, when you engage in them, bring you a sense of fulfillment and contentment.

If there are activities leftover from your week that bring anxiety, stress, or dread, then you need to think about how to flick them off your plate.

Write out:

REQUIRED   RETURN   REWARD

What's one thing can you quit today to free up more time for what God is calling you to do in your business? Sometimes we need to let go of good things in order for God to do great things in our lives. If you cannot start the goal for this principle until something else is off your plate, then that needs to be done first.

Write down how you will begin to live your goal and then write out a step-by-step plan to stop doing what is getting in the way. It may mean finding a replacement for your position or simply saying you are letting go of the responsibility.

Prayer

Lord, You have taught me that when I am doing what You desire, I have a sense of fulfillment and power. You do not promise it will be easy, but You do promise to be with me. I pray for discernment as I think through the activities I am required to do each day because of where You have me in my life. I accept that my business may look different at each stage of my life. Thank You for helping me understand my human time limitations. Help me to be all You would have me be in my required activities first. Help me see the right activities that will give me a return for Your glory. And thank You for the rewards You give me. In Jesus' name, amen.

4

The Widow in Debt: Giving All You Have

Read the Biblical account of the Widow in Debt in 2 Kings 4:1-7.

Principle: **I give God all I have for His use in my business.**

Having Nothing to Give

The Widow in Debt did not plan for this to happen to her. We meet her at a desperate time; she has two young boys and no husband. She is a single mother with no future.

Her husband, we are told, has been a part of the group of prophets who have been working with Elijah and now, Elisha (2 Kings 4:1). He had been faithful to God, but he died (we aren't told how or why), leaving her pretty much destitute. And now, the creditors are ready to take her sons as slaves to pay for her husband's debt.

She lives during a time of great turmoil. Many in the Jewish nation have fallen away from God and to make matters even crazier, Elisha is not the type of prophet to speak timidly and not tell truth. He is not exactly popular.

Do you think she blamed Elisha for her situation? I can hear one thought blaring in her head: If only we hadn't borrowed that money to live while my husband was following that man of God.

Even the most devout have their doubts when they can't understand what God is doing.

I love that she goes straight to her spiritual leader to ask for help. She reaches out to Elisha either because she blames him or because she expects him to help her. Either way, she is in front of Elisha asking for his assistance. She is bold in her request and tells it straight-forward, in a way the prophet can respect.

His response is quick and simple. He asks, "How can I help, and what do you have in your house?" (2 Kings 4:2). He appears willing to help her, but he is not going to give her a miracle like the ones he has been performing lately.

She has heard about the water filling the ditches for the army in the desert (2 Kings 3:16-17). She knows he healed the water over in Jericho, so it was potable, with just a bowl of salt (2 Kings 2:20-22). She listened to the story of the kids who made fun of him and were attacked by bears. And He wants to know what is in her house? Really?

What do you have in your house? At times it can feel like there is nothing, that you have been wrung out. After a day of work, running the kids, laundry, dinner, homework, exercise, meetings, or whatever, you are done. What is in your house? Where does God fit into all your activity?

In Hebrew, the word for widow literally means empty house. So you can see how ironic it is that Elisha asks her that question. Her immediate response is, "I have nothing." I can almost hear the irritation in her voice. Then, almost in the same breath, she says, "Well, I have a little oil."

You might feel empty, but I bet you have a little oil.

Heart Activity

Reflection Questions:

In what ways do you feel empty? What creates that state for you?

How does God fit into your daily life now? What needs to change?

Where do you turn first when you feel desperate and in need of outside help? Why?

Look back at your life. Do you have any oil? What resources has God equipped you with in order to do your business?

Prayer

Lord, thank You for never leaving me destitute. Thank You for equipping me for the job you have me doing. Help me use the gifts and expertise You have given me to do my best for You. Help me turn to You first when things are good and when things go wrong. Lord, You know what I have even when I don't see it. Give me the wisdom to turn to You and help me hear Your voice when I need it most. In Jesus' name, amen.

Giving More Than You Thought

The widow offers Elisha her little oil. I love that she offers the only thing she can think of—the only thing of value she has. Her thoughts might have been screaming, What will that little oil do?! I should save it for one last meal or for when I'm buried!

How would you respond?

God wants you to trust Him with the little things. He builds your faith on what you hold out to Him. You may feel you have nothing to offer, but you do. Think about the tasks that come easily to you. In your business, you shine in an area or two and it gives you the most joy. Give it to God for His use.

Elisha's response is not to give her a hand out; it's to give her a means of helping herself. She may have been expecting him to just perform a miracle, but God had another way to heal her heart. Elisha doesn't pity her; he gives her a plan.

Healing for her comes through action. Elisha tells her to collect from anyone and everyone as many jars and containers as she can. He gives her a project to do so she can focus on what she has, the little oil, and not on what she doesn't have. In fact, her project is so big she must include her sons—the very ones she is afraid of losing. But she trusts Elisha completely and gets to work.

Imagine the scene: the widow and her two sons going around town, knocking on doors and asking for empty containers. They may have thought crazy Elisha had rubbed off on her. There may have even been talk, laughter, and ridicule behind her back. It didn't matter to her. Her husband had believed in this man and she was honoring her husband by following his instructions.

Her job isn't hard; it is simply an act of obedience.

Sometimes we dismiss something that comes easily and naturally to us, thinking God can't or won't use it in our business. Your work doesn't always have to be hard—sometimes you just have to be obedient.

For the widow, this may be the first time she is doing anything outside of the home. The first time she has thought about how she can make money to care for her family. Elisha didn't instruct her to go get a job or go back to school to learn a trade. He asks her what she has and tells her how to use it.

Where you are now may be the first time you have thought of having your own business. It may be the first time you have thought about a way to bring in income to your household based on a passion or desire God has given to you. He is asking you to trust Him to do great things with the little you have to offer.

The Widow and her sons collect any and all containers they can borrow. The house is lined with all sorts of shapes, sizes, and colors of pottery. Elisha instructs her to go into the house and close the doors. No one is to watch them as they fill the containers from the little oil she has in her flask. This miracle is for her family only.

Her sons bring her each container and she fills each one to the brim. The task is long and arduous. Empty containers are easy to move around; full ones are not. I hope they had a system. If not, I can just see them running around checking to see if there were any more jars. (But that's just me—I would have been systematic.)

She continues the job until the last container is filled. The little oil stops flowing only when every jar is full (2 Kings 4:6). She goes directly to Elisha and tells him what happened. He instructs her to sell it all, pay back the debt, and live on the rest. A beautiful picture of God's provision.

The adage, "the more you give, the more you get" may be true, but I think it's better said like this: "The more you give God the more He can bless it." It is in our obedience to Him in the little things that we can be given larger responsibilities. God wants it all. The widow gave what she had and God multiplied it.

Hold nothing back from God. Give Him your skills, expertise, talents. Trust Him to do what He wants in your business. Even if the answers seem to take you in a direction you would have never thought about going. Trust it will work out and that He has your good at heart. Those small steps speed up and turn into leaps. Your business vision—the purpose He put in your heart—begins to flow and continues until you have filled up every container He has given you.

Soul Activity

God asks each of us to offer what we have so He can use it (Romans 12:1). Today you will be Praying in Color about giving God everything, starting with the small things in your life and working up to the larger ones. Write the word surrender either in the center of your page or at the top. Draw a bubble, cloud, or shape around the word. Color and doodle on the page. Ask God what you are not giving Him.

Start listing the little things in your life you need to surrender to God first. Examples might be your schedule, attitude toward someone, time with Him, etc. Add words that come to mind, and place them in shapes around the main word.

Add colors, lines, marks and shapes. Ask God to show you where you are empty so He can fill you up. Ask for His help to see where you need to surrender to Him. Draw the images and words He impresses on your heart.

Return to this Praying in Color activity often as a way to check how you are doing. Keep working through all the parts of your life you need to surrender to Him. Gradually grow into the big things in your life: business, marriage, family, past, etc.

Prayer

Lord, I know I have failed when it comes to surrendering all the parts of my life. I have tried, but I take things back and try to do it on my own. Thank You for making me a capable woman who can do things well. Help me rely on Your strength and not my own. Let me see You work in my life as I trust You and serve You. I pray for guidance as You search my heart and bring to the surface where I have not surrendered to You. Help me be the woman of God I am called to be by surrendering everything to You. In Jesus' name, amen.

Widow in Debt Guided Imagery

This is a guided imagery exercise. Read it through completely before you begin the activity. Refer to the instructions for creating your environment and the breathing exercise in the front of this book to begin relaxing.

After you have relaxed with the breathing, continue breathing slowly and imagine this scene:

You are laying on a comfortable chaise lounge chair. Your legs are stretched out and your feet clad in soft slippers. You are in a thick white terrycloth robe. Your hair is tied up neat in another towel. You're taking an indulgent spa day. The breeze from the garden hits your newly scrubbed face as you lie there with a cool gel mask across your eyes.

You have taken the day to get away and surrender to time alone. Time to regenerate. So far, the day has surpassed anything you could have imagined and you are calm and relaxed. The breeze brings a whiff of lavender and you inhale deeply, adding to your pleasure.

The spa attendant brings you a cool, delicious drink and lets you know it's time to move into your mud bath. As you sip the sweet contents of the glass, you walk through an arch and down a long hall. The temperature warms as you approach the door to the mud bath. This is the part of the spa you weren't so sure about. The thought of going into warm mud seems a little strange.

You open the door to find Jesus waiting for you. He sees your confusion and laughs. "I wanted to find some time to talk with you today. I thought this would be the best place. I thought you would be ready." He holds out His hand. "Do you trust me to put you in the mud?"

His presence is comforting. All day you have been trying to release your problems, trying to relax. Getting into the mud bath seems easier because He is there. You set down your drink, take off your robe, and walk over to Him. He takes your hand and guides you into the thick warm goo.

Your feet find the platform as you feel the mud squish between your toes and you walk down the small steps. Slowly the mud engulfs your body, first your legs and then your torso. Jesus motions to one end of the pit where there is a seat and you submerge up to your neck. Your body feels heavy under the mud. You move your arm from side to side and it is like moving in slow motion. Steam rises from in front of you and Jesus brings a pillow for your head.

He sits at the top of the mud bath and looks down at you. Your pillow is perfectly positioned to see Him without strain on your neck. Listen to what He wants to say to you. He wants you to surrender everything to Him much in the same way you surrendered to this spa day, even to the mud itself. Feel the weight of the mud as He mentions all the places in your life He wants you to surrender. Confess those areas of your life and talk with Him about what it might look like for you to surrender them to Him.

Allow Him to help you out of the mud. Shower and feel the newness of washing off the mud. Put on your robe, hug Jesus, and thank Him for the time of confession and freeing. Feel His forgiveness as you begin surrendering every part of your life to Him.

Lie there as long as you wish until you are ready to move. Continue breathing deeply until you want to get up and reflect.

Response Activity

Once you have completed the imagery exercise, use your journal or a piece of paper to reflect on what God revealed to you about what you need to surrender to Him. What is it like to spend time with Him? Be sure to record the feelings and thoughts you experienced as you met Jesus in the mud bath of your spa day.

Prayer

Lord, thank You for Your understanding heart. Thank You that even when I fail to do what You want, You forgive me. Open my heart to see me as You see me. Help me give everything over to You so you can use it for Your glory. Thank You for the cleansing of confession. Please keep me close to You so I am aware of You each moment of my day. Guide me to surrender all situations, attitudes, and circumstances to You. In Jesus' name, amen.

Mind Activity

Principle: **I give God all I have for His use in my business.**

After a day of kids, carpools, laundry, meal planning, cooking, cleaning, marketing, phone calls, meetings, networking, and clients you can feel a little empty. Let's face it, a lot of empty. And I forgot to mention your self-care that includes exercise, eating well, and spiritual renewal (time with God). Are you there? Do you feel that drain as you read the list? I feel the drain just writing it.

Many times you feel this way because the demands of your life have you working outside of your natural talents and strengths. How can you get all the things done you need to without feeling drained? Priorities. And, understanding what you do well and doing more of it.

You have many natural talents, things that come easily to you. You can think back over your life and see the things you enjoy and feel a real sense of pride when accomplishing. Talents also work in areas that you are good at even if it is not your favorite thing to do. If you have ever thought or said, "Let me do it for you," then it's something you're good at.

For this goal, think about what you are really good at doing. A natural talent only becomes a real strength if you practice it, develop it, and learn more about it. God wants you to take the talent He has given you and bring it into alignment with your business and calling.

Here are some questions to guide you through the thought process:

Look back: What things did you enjoy doing as a kid? What did you do a lot?

What you enjoy: What types of activities can you get lost in now? What subjects do you like to talk about with others?

What you are good at: What comes easy to you? What do people compliment you about?

Successes: What have you been successful at doing? Taken pride in? What has gotten you recognition?

Challenges: When have you risen to an occasion? What unseen skills did you use to help the situation?

Author Tom Rath's book, StrengthsFinder (and accompanying assessment), is an excellent tool in finding what you're naturally good at. You can use this resource or the above questions to list your top five talents or strengths and then write your goal to reflect giving each over to God for Him to use in your business.

Write out your Goal.

S

M

A

R

T

Here is my example: I will create more fun and interaction in my workshops by using my drama expertise. When I use this ability I am aligning with my command strength so I show up with presence.

Strength Activity

Principle: **I give all I have to God for His use in my business.**

Your action plan for this goal should include listing all your natural talents and then listing each area of your business. Identify which talents are effective in which areas of your business. Realize these are the places you can do your best and should concentrate your efforts.

This means there will be areas in your business you're not as talented and could benefit from others' talents. That's okay; this is what your network is for. Start looking for people who can fill those spaces for you because those areas are their strengths.

Begin taking actions to shift your business practices to work in your strengths. Do more of what you're good at and outsource the areas where others' talents work better.

As you grow and learn more about yourself, continue to come to God open-handed as you give back to Him each talent He brings to your attention.

Create your action plan for your goal.

Prayer

Thank You, God, for creating me uniquely. You have given me the exact combination of talents and strengths I need to live out my calling and do my business. Help me continue to give back to You each talent as I seek to build my business for You. Please bring into my life the business partners and resources I need to succeed in the business You have given me. Thank You for allowing me to serve You in this way. In Jesus' name, amen.

5

Lydia: Woman of Influence

Read the Biblical account of Lydia in Acts chapter 16.

Principle: **I have unique influence in my marketplace.**

Discovering Your Style

Lydia, the woman with her own style! Flamboyant, friendly and successful. She is the go-to woman for the finest in clothes; she knows her customers and their tastes. Lydia is the fashion mogul of her town, and I am sure she dresses the part!

This business powerhouse is only mentioned by name in two verses in the Bible, but she has an influence and reach that extends into every part of her region and to us today. We meet her in Philippi, where she conducts business. Her background gives her the right credentials to be a seller of purple cloth.

She's from Thyatira, an area famous for its technique in dying this rare cloth. There are actually two forms of purple cloth: one for royalty and one for the masses. Both techniques are laborious, but the higher quality one required more specialized materials. The knock-off brand is easier to produce because the ingredients are more readily available.

Lydia's business is lucrative, especially in the ancient world. The cloth, we are told, is worth its weight in silver. Lydia enjoys a luxurious life, I imagine, just like the fabric she sells. Purple is the color of royalty and everyone wants it. She is in high demand and everyone in her marketplace knows who she is. She has branded herself well—I'm sure her logo is purple.

I love that we never see her apologize for doing well in business and apparently having wealth. She owns a home, has her own servants, and makes all the decisions for her household. She is the whole package. And she loves God! She is a woman just like you, merging her two worlds by staying culturally relevant and positioned to share her faith.

When we first meet her in Philippi, she's sitting by the river with a group of women praying (Acts 16:13-14). She may have also memorized portions of the Pentateuch, the first five books of the Bible otherwise known to Israel as God's Law, that she could quote. We are not told how Lydia became a believer in God, Yahweh. She is named for a place, indicating she came from slavery; we can speculate she may have worked in a Jewish household and learned about God from them. But here on the riverbank, on the Sabbath, she is leading worship of the one true God.

It's Lydia's humble beginnings that draw me to her story. I look at her and see a successful woman who has worked hard to get where she is in life. No short cuts or nepotism, just brilliant business choices: from choosing a high-demand product to selecting the urban center market of Philippi as her venue. Maybe you can relate, too. Sometimes we think we cannot do a work for God because of our backgrounds. We feel others are more qualified. We think we can never measure up to His calling. But that is a lie of the enemy.

Lydia is our example to follow.

Two things happen that day on the riverbank after Paul and Silas meet the women. One, God opens Lydia's heart to accept Christ, and two, she acts immediately with the resources and skills at her disposal. She doesn't wait for permission, to take a class, or even get the approval of her customers; she believes and is baptized as well as everyone in her household (a woman in charge!). Then she invites Paul and Silas to stay in her home!

Her personality shows hospitality and generosity are part of who God created her to be. She hosts the missionaries and learns from them. She embraces the platform and wealth she has been awarded and services it for God, using the financial fruit of her business to make a difference. She is a woman of many talents— just as you are. The combination of your personal motivations and expertise gives you unique influence in the marketplace, and God wants to use it. Lydia didn't shy away from the vivacious, fun woman she really was; she embraced her passions and used them to show Christ in a way no one else could. And so can you—in a way only you can.

Heart Activity

Reflection Questions:

What is your leadership or business style and how does it make you unique in your business interactions?

What decisions have you made that resulted in creating more and better business for you?

What in your background has given you a limiting belief about yourself?

How can you use a gift or talent right now to make a difference in someone's life?

Prayer

Lord, I thank You for creating me to be unique. You have given me exactly what I need to do the work You have called me to do. I thank You for my abilities that allow me to run my business well. I thank You for my spiritual gifts, too. Help me use these Spirit-infused abilities to share You with others. Father, I know at times I limit You because I believe false limitations about myself. Help me remove the lies I sometimes believe about myself and give me new ways to think. You made me to have a unique influence in the marketplace; help me embrace it. In Jesus' name, amen.

Creating Your Own Style

Lydia is a woman with many abilities and is driven to do things in a way that works for her business. God uses it in miraculous ways. We know she is a woman of prayer (Acts 16:13). This connects her to God, allowing her to love those she encounters each day. God uses prayer to change us so we can better represent Him to those around us.

She is also a worshiper of God (Acts 16:14). Worship allows her to be aware of God throughout her entire day. She recognizes God's goodness and majesty and uses her work as worship during the week and at the riverbank on the Sabbath. She leads others into the presence of God through her own style of sociability and enthusiasm.

Lydia also displays service, hospitality, and generosity (Acts 16:15), by extending an invitation to Paul and Silas to stay in her home. Her hospitality allows them to create a hub for the budding church in Philippi (Acts 16:40). Her generosity cares for them when they are thrown in jail for disturbing the peace (Acts 16:22-24). And she serves others by being a strong leader in this new church (Philippians 1:3-5).

This combination of strong business leadership ability and her natural gifts gives Lydia a unique influence in her marketplace. As a charismatic, successful woman, she sets an example worth following. Her influence with her customers, employees, trade merchants, and vendors gives her opportunities for making disciples of Jesus. Her role is vital for her world.

And your role is vital for yours.

Your unique combination of natural abilities and motivational style is perfect for where you are in your business and for who you regularly connect with. God has given you both to work together in your marketplace endeavors. Often your natural abilities become Spirit-infused gifts to show others the glory and goodness of God. This is when you can really align your calling with your role in the marketplace. And that enables you to worship God through your work because it can produce eternal rewards and results. Amazing.

You may not be the exciting, sociable, purple-wearing Lydia, but you are exactly who you need to be. We each have our own resources and style; some of us are competitive and headstrong, others systematic and organized, while still others are loyal and great listeners. I am glad we are not made from the same mold (or, should I say, cut from the same cloth?). God is so creative, so why shouldn't His children be? Lydia's faith was expressed in her individuality and your faith needs to be expressed in your own personality and distinctiveness. That's what makes it authentic.

You are who God intended you to be! Embrace it, own it, and be authentic. Open your heart, give your resources, and keep your style. It is your unique influence in the marketplace that God will use.

Soul Activity

God's has created you with a unique motivation to shine in your business Today you will be Praying in Color about the things that are important to you in the way you do your business. In the center of your page write down the word Motivates.

Draw a bubble, cloud, or shape around the word. Continue to color and doodle on the page. Create a mind map of sorts by brainstorming and writing down the things that are most important to you in your business. Write them in shapes around the main word and look to see what behaviors drive you in your business.

Add other colors, lines, marks and shapes. Ask God to show you how your unique style motivates you to show up in your business and how it can create your unique influence in the marketplace. Draw the images and write the words He impresses on your heart.

If there is anything in your past getting in the way of your belief in your abilities or gifts, ask God to remove it and forgive you for believing the lies of the devil. Ask Him to give you faith to believe what He says about you.

Prayer

God, You are so creative. Thank You for using Your creativity on me as You put together my unique abilities and gifts. I am the combination You designed so I could be the influence You want me to be in my business. I love how You have created me to be Your representative in my sphere of influence. Help me share my gifts and abilities with others so they see You in my life. In Jesus' name, amen.

Lydia Guided Imagery

This is a guided imagery exercise. Read it through completely before you begin the activity. Refer to the instructions for creating your environment and the breathing exercise in the front of this book to begin relaxing.

After you have relaxed with the breathing, continue to breathe slowly and imagine this scene:

It's early evening. You are walking on an ancient dirt road toward a low, single-story house surrounded by a low stone wall. There is a wooden double door on iron hinges at the entrance. You move down the road toward the door. The sun is low in the sky casting deep shadows across the fields around the home.

This is Lydia's house. You can hear people talking and laughing in the courtyard. You knock on the door and a young boy answers. He welcomes you in and directs you to the tables and benches set up around an inviting fire.

Lydia's household is buzzing with activity. You walk closer to the fire and feel its warmth on your face as you stretch your hands out to warm them. You watch as servants rush around, bringing food and drink to the tables. They are happy to be serving on this occasion.

You look toward the wall of the house and see Lydia seated with a woman in deep prayer. You look in the other direction and see a group of men encouraging another man who looks distraught. There are lots of back slaps and hugs.

The sun has gone down completely now and it's getting dark except for the fire. You move toward another group with women. The older women in the group are teaching the younger ones a new technique for embroidering onto Lydia's purple fabric. Everyone seems to be enjoying the interaction; smiling, they invite you to join them. You sit down on the hard wooden bench as everyone at the table moves closer together to make room for you.

You are witnessing a gathering of the early church, with each person bringing their uniqueness to the setting. Feel the compassion they have for one another. Look around and see their care for one another. Lydia comes into view from the firelight and invites everyone to bow in prayer.

As she prays, the woman beside you grasps your hand, and you realize Lydia is praying for strength for each of them to be who God calls them to be in their businesses, their work, their day-to-day lives. You feel the woman's love through her hand as she squeezes ever so slightly.

Lydia prays for them to have unity and to tell others about Jesus in their own unique way. The woman next to you places her other hand on top of yours and you feel strengthened. You know God has called you to use your own style and uniqueness for Him. The fire crackles as Lydia continues praying. You are filled with awe as you see all the care and acceptance displayed in this court-yard. You feel a part of something bigger than yourself and you are excited to contribute.

Lie there as long as you wish until you are ready to move. Continue breathing deeply until you want to get up and reflect.

Response Activity

Once you have completed the imagery exercise, use your journal or paper to reflect on what God revealed to you about using your unique style and personality for Him in your marketplace. Be sure to record the feelings and thoughts you experienced as you watched God's gifts being used at Lydia's house.

Prayer

Father, thank You for revealing to me that I am uniquely designed by You with a personality and style that is assigned only to me. I understand I am to use my style in my marketplace each day. By being my authentic self, I can worship you in spirit and in truth (John 4:23). Help me live as an authentic, inspired believer in You. In Jesus' name, amen.

Mind Activity

Principle: **I have unique influence in my marketplace.**

Connecting to your own style can be a challenge because we always want to be like someone else who we see as successful. But only you can show up as you in your business and life. God never asks us to change our personalities, but He does change us. He gave you your eye and hair color as well as the shape of your face and body. Celebrate your differences. Celebrate that only you can bring into the world the ideas He is giving you. Thank Him that He has entrusted you with this important task.

To create your goal for this principle, we will look at how you are motivated in your work. There is a distinct way you approach your work. In fact, there are four style categories people fall into: Dominant, Influence, Steadiness, and Conscientious.

These categories are from the DiSC® Behavioral Assessment. I have come to use this tool because of its effectiveness in determining the motivations of myself and others in business and it allows me to work with and communicate better with others because I am aware of our differences. No one personality is better or more effective than the other in order to be successful in business. They are behavior styles, when understood, help you know how to be more effective in your dealings with customers, business partners, co-workers, and employees.

There are various DiSC® assessments you can take online. Make sure there is a lower-case 'i' in the acronym to get the real thing. Once you have determined where you fall in the DiSC® assessment, write your goal based on what behaviors are important in your business and how you will show up that way.

Write out your Goal.

S

M

A

R

T

Here is an example: So I can work more effectively with my team during this project, I will watch each person's body language and listen for clue words to understand their motivational style and adjust my style to meet theirs for better rapport and communication.

Strength Activity

Principle: **I have unique influence in my marketplace.**

Now it is your turn to pull out the information you know about your style and what motivates you in business and put it into an action plan so you can live out the goal. Think about the people you have dealings with each day or each week. Decide how you can begin to embrace your own style and use it to be more effective with others. Describe five or six situations where you can implement it and show up with your personal style.

Incorporate this type of thinking as you work with others in the future on different business goals. Since you are aware of this tool, it is your responsibility to use it to communicate with your unique style and influence in the marketplace.

Prayer

Lord, You have given me all the tools I need to do the work You have designed for me. Thank You for my uniqueness and for the opportunity to use it in my work. I pray for guidance as I implement my personal style and motivation in my business. I ask that You help me see how I can be Your representative in the marketplace by using my unique style and influence. Thank You for this opportunity. In Jesus' name, amen.

6

Priscilla:
Building Relationships
That Matter

Read the Biblical account of Priscilla in Acts chapter 18.

Principle: **I serve God and others by developing relationships in the marketplace.**

Strategic Relationships

Strong-minded, enthusiastic in her love for God and Jesus, loyal to her husband, and a mover and a shaker—this is Priscilla. She is mentioned six times in the Bible, each time alongside her husband, Aquila. They were a power couple in business and in the Church. Imagine Paul's surprise to meet followers of Jesus in Corinth—a commercial city with two waterfronts, known for its rough characters and loose morals.

Priscilla lives and works in Corinth, but she is really a Roman Jew.

Apparently, Emperor Claudius has thrown out all the Jews from Rome, even prominent ones like Priscilla and Aquila. They work in leather, making tents and other goods. Upon meeting Paul, Priscilla invites him to stay with them because they have the same profession! So begins a business relationship as well as a spiritual friendship.

I imagine Priscilla learned even more about Jesus under Paul's teaching. Every Sabbath, he would go to the synagogue and persuade Jews and Greeks to follow "The Way." (Acts 18:4) I'm sure she also invited people to come with her to hear about Jesus.

It's important to remember the Church is just beginning. Everyone is integral to the success of spreading the news of Jesus Christ. Today, it's the same; we each have the responsibility to share Jesus. When Silas and Timothy arrive, Priscilla has even more believers for support and encouragement. Building relationships with other believers—within the Church as well as in the marketplace—is crucial to the work God has for us.

After a while, though, the Jews in Corinth no longer want Paul in the synagogue. But many have believed and the Church is growing. Priscilla now opens her home for the teaching of the Gospel. Paul stays in Corinth, preaching and teaching, for the next year and a half.

Priscilla and Aquila serve in many capacities within the early Church. Working together with Paul creates friendship bonds. Since Paul and Priscilla worked day-in and day-out together, the friendship grows and deepens. I'm sure working together to bring others to Christ added a level of care and respect for one another, too. These bonds of friendship greatly enrich Paul and his ministry. Here in Corinth, Priscilla and Aquila become some of Paul's closest friends, leaders in the faith, and part of his inner circle.

As a couple, Priscilla and Aquila complement one another. Not compliment, like a positive statement about someone, but complement, a fitting together or accompanying or completing each other. She is definitely the extrovert of the couple; Aquila is much more reserved. She is the front-of-the-store type, dealing with customers, while he is more about the process and quality control; he's a making-sure-projects-get-done kind of guy. I like how this couple is interdependent on one another, each working in their own strengths. That's what makes them successful both in business and as leaders in the church.

Our workplace can be like this as well. By working together, we build relationships with people in our offices, in our networking groups, and in other business dealings. This provides an opportunity for us to connect with other believers for mutual support—a support system that allows us to serve others in the marketplace in order to show them Christ.

As a strong woman, Priscilla could be intimidating to others. But that is not something she is concerned with because she is all about serving others and sharing Christ. Along with her husband, she teaches about Jesus and the Gospel, hosts the church in her home, and leads by example. Though they have all this going for them, the couple is content to let others shine. It is all about community and developing lasting relationships that matter.

Heart Activity

Reflection Questions:

How have relationships with other believers in the marketplace encouraged and supported you in your faith?

Who has God placed in your business life with whom you want to develop a deeper friendship? Why?

How can you serve others through your business so you can build more relationships?

Prayer

Lord, I come before You and thank You for my business. Thank You for the opportunities to meet new people and build relationships. Father, help me serve the people I meet each day in a way that brings us closer. I pray for guidance to know who to invest my time in and develop relationships that matter. Help me connect with other believers in the marketplace for support and encouragement and help me be the same for them. In Jesus' name, amen.

Relationship Roles

Paul, Priscilla, and her husband leave Corinth and go to Ephesus together. Paul leaves them in charge to continue the work in Ephesus as the spiritual leaders of the church. Soon, Apollos, a great preacher, comes and tells about the coming Messiah. Apollos is well-spoken and many listen. He, however, only knows what John the Baptist preached about Jesus and repentance (Acts 18:25). He has never been told about Jesus and salvation through His shed blood and baptism based on faith; he only has part of the story.

Priscilla is gracious with her words whenever she gives instruction and correction, and I suspect Aquila to be the same. The couple invites Apollos to their home after listening to his speech at the synagogue and explain the entire Gospel to him (Acts 18:26). Priscilla is a mentor with true humility and tact. Apollos is appreciative for her insights and knowledge and uses his new information to debate with the Jews he meets in the future (Acts 18:28).

God shows us through Priscilla's example how He uses simple, hard-working women and men to move His work forward.

He wants to use you, too.

While in Ephesus, Priscilla is privileged to be part of training Timothy, a young and faithful disciple who becomes a dynamic leader. Pouring into the younger generation is natural for Priscilla. I think this mentor relationship may have been one of her favorite parts of her work. Her heart is to nourish and support the friends and workers in the faith she encounters through her business. The church in Ephesus thrives under the leadership of Priscilla and her husband.

Soon it is time to leave Ephesus. In the first century, it is not uncommon for the Jews in commercial industries to move along the trade routes and follow the markets. Priscilla gets the opportunity to return to Rome after the death of Claudius. I have to imagine she was eager to reconnect with old friends and catch up with extended family.

When Priscilla returns to Rome, she is a different person. Priscilla may have met Paul as a follower of Jesus, but now she is a true disciple, mentor, and leader. Their travels have made her and Aquila stronger and wiser, and their faith is deeper and wider. Both have experienced God working in His people in miraculous ways. They have lived through many experiences both good and bad. The early church suffered through times of persecution and rejoiced in times of great flourishing. Priscilla and Aquila witnessed it all and have built deep, meaningful friendships that will last a lifetime. Working together for a common goal will do that.

The tent-making business supports Priscilla's work in the early Church. It allows her and her husband to work without burdening anyone for the ministry part of their lives. It also gives them opportunities to meet many different people, develop friendships, and introduce them to Jesus. For Priscilla, it is all about building networks, investing in lives, and sharing the love of Jesus.

When Paul writes the letter to the Roman church, it is delivered to Priscilla's house, where the church meets. In it, he equates Priscilla's help to the work of Timothy and Titus. Her contribution is as an equal partner in business and in the leadership of the church (Romans 16:3).

Her story doesn't end in Rome; Priscilla is last seen in Ephesus (2 Timothy 4:19). Building a business, building relationships, building a life of service never ends. Retirement is not an option for Priscilla and she is happy to serve alongside her husband. Together, they inspire and equip leaders, instruct and cultivate disciples, invest and train believers, and introduce new friends to Jesus. It's an exciting life, a life of service. It's a life of developing relationships that matter.

Soul Activity

God places people in your path everyday through your business. Who comes to mind when you think about work relationships? Today you will be Praying in Color about the people God wants you to be involved with and be encouraged by, and those with whom He wants you to share Jesus.

In your journal or on a piece of paper, list two people you know who are believers in the faith with whom you can develop relationships for mutual encouragement. Then list two people God puts on your heart to develop your friendship with in a more meaningful and direct way so you may eventually tell them about Christ. Next to each person, jot down the reason these people may have come to mind. Next, take a few moments to pray for each person and ask God how to approach each relationship. Pray for each person separately. Prayer is the best place to start when developing relationships that matter. (Use the space below your list to do this activity.)

Write each name somewhere on the page.

Draw a bubble, cloud, or shape around the name.

Add color, lines, and words around each person's name as you think about them. Ask God to show you their needs and how you can best pray for them. Ask God to show you how to serve them.

Draw the images and/or write the words He impresses on your heart

As you move on to the next name, breathe an amen and continue until all four have been prayed over.

Prayer

Father, You fill me with awe when I think about the ways You can use me to further Your kingdom. I want to be used by You to make Your name famous. Help me build lasting relationships that bring me and others closer to You. I love You and I am excited to be able to show Your love to others through my relationships and through my work. Please give me courage to continue the work You have started in me. In Jesus' name, amen.

Priscilla Guided Imagery

This is a guided imagery exercise. Read it through completely before you begin the activity. Refer to the instructions for creating your environment and the breathing exercise in the front of this book to begin relaxing.

After you have relaxed with the breathing, continue to breathe slowly and imagine this scene:

You are sitting at a corner table in a coffee shop. To your left there is a long wall with photos of coffee cups, coffee beans, and mountains where coffee grows. It's a cold and cloudy day; the windows across from you look opaque instead of clear with the clouds against them.

The aroma of freshly brewed coffee is pungent in the air. You sit with your favorite warm drink in front of you. Take a sip and feel the warmth of the fluid as it fills your mouth and slides into your body. It fills you with relief and tastes perfect.

Look around the room. You are almost alone. Feel the wooden chair under your thighs. It is hard and sturdy and you are aware of its support as you lean back. You hear the soft melody of a song playing in the background, but you don't recognize it.

Then you see her enter. It's Priscilla. She sees you and waves as she goes to order her coffee. You are meeting with her today for your first mentoring session. Your stomach is a little nervous; you aren't sure what to expect.

You move forward and slide your fingers across the table and feel the grooves and imperfections in the wood. Priscilla comes, sits, and smiles at you. Her eyes are friendly and you immediately relax. She came to help you think through some things. She's here to guide you.

You circle your hands around your cup and let its heat warm your hands. Then you begin. Tell Priscilla how you want to be used by God through your relationships. Ask about her experiences of serving others. Share your heart with her and hear her advice. She will stay at the coffee shop for as long as you need.

Listen for what God may be saying to your heart through Priscilla's.

Lie there as long as you wish until you are ready to move. Continue breathing deeply until you want to get up and reflect.

Response Activity

Once you have completed the guided imagery exercise, use your journal or a piece of paper to reflect on what God revealed to you about building relationships and serving others in your marketplace. Be sure to record the feelings and thoughts you experienced as you shared with and listened to Priscilla.

Prayer

God, You amaze me each day. I am grateful for the relationship I have with You. Help me connect with other believers in my marketplace for friendship and encouragement. Please bless those relationships as we work in our businesses and for You. Give me the courage to develop relationships with others so I can share You with them. Give me a heart to serve in the marketplace so others see Your goodness and love. In Jesus' name, amen.

Mind Activity

Principle: **I serve God and others by developing relationships in the marketplace.**

The Soul Activity earlier helped you discover two and two: Two people who could come alongside you and be an encouragement and source of support, and two people God put on your heart to begin a relationship with to eventually share Jesus.

Building supportive relationships is essential for your business and ministry. You are never alone. God brings others into your life to give you strength and encouragement to do what He has called you to do.

Again, your workplace gives you an ideal place to start. Through work you build relationships with people in your office, in your networking groups, and in other business settings. You connect with other believers for mutual support so you can serve others in the marketplace and show them Christ.

It does not stop there though. As you work through your goal for this principle, start with the two and two God revealed to you in the Soul Activity. Then create your goal around HOW you will continue to use the two and two technique. This is not a static list; continually add people to the list in both areas: believers for support and non-believers for opportunities to share.

The goal can be as specific or as general as you want. This goal should become your mode of operation as you live out the Great Commission (Matthew 28:16-20).

Write out your Goal.

S

M

A

R

T

Here is an example: I will develop relationships in the marketplace with believers and non-believers by using the two-and-two method. With other believers, I will develop a support system for our mutual benefit as we strive to share Jesus. With non-believers I will pray for, start, and continue relationships, and share Jesus so they can become disciples, too.

Strength Activity

Principle: **I serve God and others by developing relationships in the marketplace.**

Creating an action plan for this goal can be straight-forward. Begin with prayer for the people God has already revealed to you. Next, brainstorm ways to start these relationships or deepen the ones you already have.

Remember, relationships are a messy business and there will be times when it will be difficult. God provides His people for that reason. Be sure to continually add like-minded believers to your circle so you have the support you need for the work God has for you and reaching out to others.

Develop a strategy so this goal does not become stagnant. You are never done telling others about Jesus. Simply show Jesus in your relationships, and build trust with people so you can speak about Him.

Write out a strategy that will support your goal:

Prayer

Lord, thank You for the example of Priscilla. She is a perfect model of building relationships that matter. Help me reach out to the other Christians in my work who can support and encourage me. Also, help me to begin real relationships with the two people You have put on my heart. Please help me be a support to my fellow believers as we live out the Great Commission together. I thank You for the opportunity to serve You by sharing Jesus with people through my work. Give me courage to do Your will. In Jesus' name, amen.

7

Puah & Shiphrah: Work for God, Not for Men

Read the Biblical account of Puah and Shiphrah in Exodus 1:6-22.

Principle: **I practice doing what is right regardless of the consequences.**

Do Your Best Because It Is Right

God's plans for greatness seem to always begin with women, and this is what we see with two midwives who had courage and dedication to their profession. Puah and Shiphrah are leaders in their industry and the main teachers of their craft. They are also the catalysts for the Exodus story in the Bible.

Here's their spot in history: The Israelites have been in Egypt for 300 years, give or take. Jacob, Joseph, and his brothers have all died, as well as their children, grandchildren, and great grandchildren. But the 70 members of Jacob's clan have now grown to over two million: the Israelites.

When they first arrived in Egypt, they were given the choicest land—Goshen. They were guests of an Egyptian Pharaoh who favored Joseph. Now, all these years later, the situation has changed. The current Pharaoh does not see a people whom they welcomed because of Joseph, but a people who are growing faster than the Egyptians. Pharaoh feels a threat to national security.

This is where we find Puah and Shiphrah. The Israelites have been turned into slaves. The noble trades that once gave them a way to make a living have now been turned into slave labor. They're creating Pharaoh's pyramids and tombs as well as the irrigation systems and working the farm fields off the Nile.

Have you ever been in a situation where everything was great at the beginning but then something happened that drastically changed the atmosphere? It may have been too subtle to notice right away, or it could have been an event where you just knew it would be different from then on. That's where the Israelites are: a situation they did not plan for or expect.

But God...

Even though the Israelites are living in bitter conditions, they thrive and keep growing in numbers. Puah and Shiphrah are the leading midwives for both the Hebrew and Egyptian women. They are sought-after in both nations because they are the best in their field. Certainly, they teach and train others because there is no way two women could do all the work. They are not only bosses but icons in midwifery.

Wouldn't that be a great place to be in your industry? At the top of your game and being recognized for it? That's exactly where Puah and Shiphrah are. But for them, life is not perfect. Neither have children of their own, not uncommon for midwives. In fact, many women entered this type of work so they could find their place in a society that valued family.

These women know what it means to sacrifice comfort, time, and resources to get the job done. They are strong in their skills and their faith (Exodus 1:17). Hardship is the way of life for the Israelites, yet they meet every opportunity to work with excellence in whatever God has called them to do.

Meanwhile, Pharaoh has tried for years to create an environment that would stifle the population growth for the Israelites. At least that's what he thought he was doing. He is threatened by the huge population living right there in the Nile River Basin with him. Interestingly, he isn't worried about an Israelite rebellion; he's more concerned they would join forces with anyone trying to attack Egypt.

Since that tactic hasn't worked, his next plan is to get rid of the threat at its source: no boys being born means no men growing up to fight.

So Pharaoh calls—no, demands—Puah and Shiphrah before him. He has devised a disturbing plan to rid himself of the threat of "these Hebrews" (Exodus 1:10). He burdens them with a horrific task, the very antithesis of their job and purpose. He orders them to kill all the Hebrew male children as they are being born. As soon as they see it is a boy, they are to destroy the child.

Puah and Shiphrah are faced with a decision that may have dire consequences: Obey Pharaoh or obey God?

Heart Activity

Reflection Questions:

Describe a time when a situation turned from a good opportunity to something you did not expect. What was your reaction?

Who are the superstars in your industry? Are you jealous of them? Or do you admire them? What do you know about their story and what they sacrificed to get there?

If you had to choose between doing what the government or your boss and what God wanted, what would you do? What consequences would you most fear?

Has there been a time in your life when you knew the right thing to do but there were circumstances that gave you pause or caused concern? Describe what happened. What would you do differently?

Prayer

Dear Lord, thank You for my business. You have given me a way to help and support others through it. Thank You for the opportunities You give me to move my business forward. Help me make wise decisions no matter the consequences. I pray to do what is right. Please help me not compare where You have placed me in my industry with anybody else. Help me be my best exactly where You have me. In Jesus' name, amen.

Do Your Best Because It's What's Needed

Puah's and Shiphrah's decision is easy. They fear God more than Pharaoh, so they decide not to do what they had been instructed

(Exodus 1:17). Imagine the most powerful man in the most powerful country gives you a direct order and you ignore it. Why? Because you fear God more than you fear him.

This fear of God isn't a terrifying fear; it's an understanding of who God is and what He asks of each of us. Reverence, respect, and awe are all words to describe this type of fear. Egyptians give this type of fear to Pharaoh, a mere man. Puah and Shiphrah give it to the one true God. Their worship is reserved for the One who holds the universe in His hands, not to the man commanding them to murder.

Standing before Pharaoh I can see their eyes meeting in horror as they think about what he is expecting them to do. If they do not obey Pharaoh, it could mean painful deaths for both of them. What could they possibly do against such a powerful man? How could they save the boys from such a terrible fate? These questions probably cross their minds as they leave Pharaoh and discuss their options in private.

We are not told exactly how they planned to get away with letting the babies live.

But we can speculate...

Since they were leaders, they needed to have a plan that included orders for every midwife in their organization. Imagine that business strategy meeting! Whiteboard (well, papyrus) out to brainstorm ideas for how to disperse the information to all their employees (midwives); an email campaign (okay, word of mouth) to explain the situation to everyone; and creating a fan base that would do what they instructed (all mothers with newborn boys).

Talk about a business explosion—their sphere of influence suddenly encompasses the entire nation of Israel. Wow! Everyone is listening to what they are saying and following their lead. There would be no killing of the baby boys on the birthing stool. The mothers are instructed to hold no birth celebrations nor draw attention to circumcision ceremonies. Everything would be covert, from pregnancy through delivery and more. This is the first time civil disobedience is recorded in Scripture. Puah and Shiphrah created the resistance.

Your sphere of influence may grow, too, as you stand up for what is right despite the consequences. God is looking for you to stand up for what is right, what He has put in your heart to do. As you trust Him with each step, each little task He asks you to do, your influence increases. What may have started out as an idea for a small business to make some extra money connects you to opportunities that propel your business forward in ways you never imagined.

Puah and Shiphrah experience an incredible surge in influence and leadership. The Israelite population continues to grow, of course, as they defy Pharaoh. All the Hebrew midwives follow their orders and the mothers follow theirs, too. It takes about a year or more for the Pharaoh to get word that there are several toddling boys down in Goshen. Furious, he calls the women before him.

They knew this day would come. They are prepared with what to say—part of the strategic plan. Pharaoh asks why they have allowed the boys to live. Puah and Shiphrah say the Hebrew women are basically like animals and can give birth without them, unlike the Egyptian flowers who need their assistance. This explanation satisfies Pharaoh and they are released.

These two women unwittingly usher in the deliverance of the Hebrews from Egypt. When Pharaoh devises an even more ruthless plan to rid himself of the Hebrew boys (Exodus 1:22), the practices implemented by Puah and Shiphrah are followed by Jochebed, who hides her son, Moses, from destruction in the Nile River. Moses, of course, would grow up to lead Israel out of Egypt.

God rewards these brave business leaders with the thing most precious to them: children of their own. Doing the right thing is more important than doing what is expected. Consequences may look dire, but God has a plan and you are part of it, even if you can't see it right now.

Soul Activity

God's plans for greatness often begin with women. Puah and Shiphrah remind us no profession is too small or too big for God to use. They were the deliverers of the deliverer of their people— Moses. Ironic that God chose to show us their story so we could hear one of the most important stories in history, God saving His people.

In your business, you are faced with decisions every day that may have small and big consequences. Knowing God has you in His plan and that He will help you make those decisions is comforting. Discerning the right thing to do is sometimes simple when the choice is black-and-white. Other times, it is in choosing what is better or best. Remember, God allows that discomfort because it forces you to seek Him for the answer.

Today you will be Praying in Color about making the right decision even when there may be consequences. In your journal or on your paper, write the word Decisions at the center. Draw a bubble, cloud, or shape around the word. Think about recent decisions you've made and their results. Ask God to recall examples for you and write these around the word. Add words, colors and shapes as

He helps you look at past decisions. Connect any consequences to specific decisions, good or bad.

On the opposite side of the page, write the word Decisions again. Draw a bubble, cloud, or shape around the word. This time, think about decisions you need to make right now. Write them spaciously around the word and allow your hand to doodle. Attach to each decision the worst consequence you can think could happen, those "what if..." thoughts. Give each worry over to God. Lift it from the page to His throne. Ask Him to speak to your heart about the right answer for this problem. Thank Him for helping you make the right decision.

Add colors, lines, marks, and shapes. Ask God for wisdom to keep your focus on what is right. Draw the images or words He impresses on your heart as He reveals a method of discernment that works for you.

Prayer

Father, You are so good to me. You have given me a great mind capable of making good decisions. Help me make the right choices each time. God, You gave me the business I have and I want to live in Your truth. Give me a way to look at problems through Your eyes and see the correct way to go. Help me not fear the consequences, but trust You for the result. In Jesus' name, amen.

Puah & Shiphrah Guided Imagery

This is a guided imagery exercise. Read it through completely before you begin the activity. Refer to the instructions for creating your environment and the breathing exercise in the front of this book to begin relaxing.

After you have relaxed with the breathing, continue to breathe slowly and imagine this scene:

You enter the dark auditorium from the back. The space is empty and the air is cool. As you walk forward, the light splashing in from the entrance dims and your eyes adjust to the darkness. At the front of the room is the stage. There is a single light shining down from somewhere above at the center. You slowly walk past the rows and rows of chairs and put your hand out to gently touch each seat as you go by.

You stop and look over the entire auditorium. Your eyes scan the first level with its rows, sections, and aisles. Looking up toward the back of the room, you see the second level with more seating. The room is voluminous and so quiet you can hear the low hum of the air conditioning.

You're here early; you wanted to get a feel for the space before you give your speech, but the event is getting closer, and people slowly start to trickle in and choose their seats. Hear the murmur of the audience as it swells and fills the space.

Your stomach flutters with eager anticipation as you see the crowd grow larger and larger, filling the seats. You prepare to go on stage. Finally, the emcee reads the introduction paragraph you provided and it's go time. You stand, find the stairs on the side, and climb them to the stage.

You walk across the matted black floor and step into the spotlight. The light is strong and you wince a little at its brightness. There's no podium; it's just you and the audience in this huge room. This is your time. You are going to speak your truth from this stage. You are going to tell others about what you do and how you want to serve them.

Your eyes adjust to the spotlight, and as you stand there, you look down at the front row, right at the center. You notice a familiar face there, one you are delighted to see. Jesus. He is here to support you, no matter how many people have come to see you. He's waiting to hear your speech, to see you shine. Your heart swells with courage as you see the pride in His eyes.

This is just the beginning of the journey for you. Look into Jesus' eyes and see Him smile at you. He is there to listen. This speech is for Him. He has been preparing you for it for a long time and you are quivering with expectation to share the message He has given you.

By now, the room is packed with your perfect audience and they are listening, hanging on your every word. But you are speaking to Jesus. To you, He's the only person in the room. Your audience of one.

Feel the heat from the light as you continue your talk. Finish and walk off the stage as the audience applauds, and go kneel at Jesus' feet. Take His hand and thank Him for this truth you get to share. Feel His hand touch your head and see Him smile at you. Tell Him all this is for Him and thank Him for your part in fulfilling His calling for your life.

Lie there as long as you wish until you are ready to move. Continue breathing deeply until you want to get up and reflect.

Response Activity

Once you have completed the imagery exercise, use your journal to reflect on what God revealed to you about speaking your truth. What is the one thing you are bringing into the world? What is the message He has for you? Does it scare you to be in front of crowds? Ask God for the strength to do what you cannot. Record the feelings and thoughts you experienced as you spoke to Jesus. What did He say as you knelt at His feet? God will give you the words you need to bring your message to those you serve through your business.

Prayer

Lord, You are always with me. Thank You. I know I will be sharing my message with many people and on many stages. Help me always remember it is to an audience of One that I am speaking. Guide me to tell others about how You have designed me to serve them. Thank You for giving me this special calling that is perfect for me. Keep me in the center of Your will so I am always connected to the Source of all good. Lord, keep me calm and moving in the direction You have for me. In Jesus' name, amen.

Mind Activity

Principle: **I practice doing what is right regardless of the consequences.**

Puah and Shiphrah had a belief system that valued human life and feared God above all else. These were personal values for both of them. Values are those ideas and beliefs that are important to you. Think about what you believe and what you stand for. Consider your convictions and what is most important in your life.

Many organizations have a value statement that expresses the various principles the business or organization stands for and how they want to appear in the public eye. These two midwives displayed their "company" values by their words and actions.

Values are also a great filtering tool for the decision-making process. By identifying those things that are most important in your life, you can decide what things get to stay on your proverbial plate and what items can be removed without guilt.

There is great power in knowing your values and then communicating them to those around you in business, work, and life. Values matter because what you consider important guides your behavior and decisions.

Your values are usually reflected at three times: when you are your happiest, when you feel the most proud, and when you are the most satisfied or fulfilled.

For this Goal, you may have to dig deep and decide what is important for you. A quick search on the internet finds many exercises with words you can use to discover your values. It's best to narrow your value words to between three and six. Personally, I have five. If an opportunity or choice does not align with any one of my values, I do not say yes.

Understanding your values allows you to feel the conviction to know when something is right for you and for what God wants you to do. It helps you make the better or best choice instead of just a good choice. Your goal should reflect HOW you are going to use your values in order to practice doing right.

Write out your Goal.

S

M

A

R

T

Here is an example: When an opportunity arises for me to make a decision that will affect my business I will use the Value's filter tool to decide if it is right for me. I will create a list of my five values and write out how the choice aligns with what I value. This will help me determine if it is something I should pursue or not.

Strength Activity

Principle: **I practice doing what is right regardless of the consequences.**

To create an action plan for this goal, first list your values in order of importance. Your aim is to honor your values when deciding what to do about your business, critiquing an opportunity, or planning something new. This list becomes a decision-making filter.

Write your 3-6 Values.

Now, create a go-to system for making decisions; this is your strategy for choosing which opportunities to take on and which to let go. This could be a flow chart or a simple list of questions related to each value. Live out your goal by using the strategy you set up for yourself.

Prayer

Lord, You are the One who created the values I hold. Thank You for giving me purpose and a way to live out exactly what is right for me. You call each of us to something different and I thank You for what you have assigned to me. Help me use my values' system to make decisions that are right for me. Help me always include You in my deliberations as I use my values to filter what I should say YES to and what I should say NO to. I trust You, Lord, to bring opportunities into my life so I can live out the goal of doing what is right no matter the consequences. In Jesus' name, amen.

8

Rahab:
Trusting God for the Results

Read the Biblical account of Rahab in Joshua chapters 2 and 6.

Principle: **My business moves forward because I trust God for who He is.**

A Woman with a Plan

Are you surprised that Rahab is included in our lineup of working women in the Bible? She is the proverbial "working girl"; Rahab was a prostitute. She was the first Gentile believer in Jehovah-God and she has a few more surprises for you too.

Rahab's story starts with rumors and reports. Not unusual for her line of work, I suppose. The Israelites have been wandering for 40 years in the desert. Their fame, or should I say God's fame, has gone before them. Everyone in the region has heard the stories of how they crossed the Red Sea on dry land and how they defeated the powerful Amorite kings on the east side of the Jordan (Joshua 2:10). The entire town of Jericho, Rahab's town, knows they are the first major city on the west side of the Jordan and the Israelites are poised and ready to cross. Every resident in Jericho is living in terror that the Israelites will destroy them.

This is where we meet Rahab. She is described in many commentaries as a hard-working business woman. Yes, she is labeled a harlot, but she also has a place for travelers to stay. She owns a home in a strategic location: the city wall. She has the attention of the king, so she must have a somewhat respected reputation. But if truth be told, she knows what she does for a living is not acceptable. Even with connections in the community, she probably feels on the fringe of society.

We all feel like this at times, right? Let's face it: her situation is like yours if you have a work environment where you are controlled by your boss and stuck in a position where you are devalued. And we have all played the recording in our heads that if someone finds out that one thing about me, they won't accept me or like me. I imagine Rahab feels stuck, with no way out. And now, with the Jews on the doorstep, she has nowhere to turn.

But Rahab is a woman with a plan. This industrious, hard-working, multi-hat-wearing woman has a plan. Maybe it was motivated by fear, but I think she was motivated by what she heard God could do. I imagine her sitting on her roof, scutching the flax she had laid out to dry and formulating what she would do—if she had the chance to escape—how she could save herself and her family. As she scraped the wooden knife along the long strands of flax, a plan emerged. She prepared for an opportunity; she just didn't know when or how it would happen. How do I know? It's evident in her quick and decisive actions when she hides the spies and then lies to the king's men. She made the decision to trust God before she even really knew who He was. At the least, she recognized there was something greater than her and she feared it. She was watching and expecting God to move and had already decided to follow Him when He did.

If God acted swiftly and powerfully in your life right now, would you be ready?

Even though Rahab has a lot going for her—multiple sources of income, leading her household, resources at her disposal, respect, and connections at the highest level in community—I am sure she is miserable. Prostitution is degrading, and I bet she saw hope in the Jews. She begs God for a way out, for a new life. Her diligent, hard-working, entrepreneurial spirit has dreams and she is ready for a change, a chance to move beyond her circumstances. It isn't a passive thought of wanting something to change, but an active, engaging, action-oriented desire for change. That's why she has prepared. She is ready to risk what is necessary to live a different life. She looks to the future with no regret.

How many times do we wait for the right sign, the right circumstance, the right feeling to move? Rahab trusts God first and decides to risk everything even before she knows if the spies will help her. You may not be a prostitute on the verge of your city's destruction, but if you are wanting, needing, to make a change and don't know where to start, Rahab's story of deliverance is relevant to you.

Her trust in God is real. Rahab believes in God's power more than in her power and puts her faith in His power. She knows she cannot control this situation or rely on her own strength to help her survive. She sees a BIG God and is overwhelmed with fear (the good kind) by what He has done. Her actions are courageous and she is given supernatural faith to stand on the side of God's people.

Using faith in your business means you are looking to God to do big things. Trust God to give you exactly what you need, when you need it. He'll help you do exactly what He wants you to do to move forward and make a change in your business.

Heart Activity

Reflection Questions:

What change do you want God to do in your business?

What plans and preparations are you making to move forward?

What is the BIG dream you need faith and trust in God to make happen?

How are you trusting God with taking risks in your business?

Prayer

Lord, I thank You for saving me through the blood of Your son, Jesus. You began a work in my life by giving me the Holy Spirit to guide me. You gave me faith when I believed—thank You. Rahab has reminded me that You are a powerful God who reached out to me in my circumstance and gave me new life. She trusted You with her dreams and plans, and I trust You with mine. Help me be bold for You, Lord. Move me forward in my business because I trust in You. In Jesus' name, amen.

The Plan Executed

The men who come to check out the city of Jericho are given a place to stay for the night by Rahab. Can you imagine God's elect rushing into a home on the wall of the city because it is an inn, trying to be discreet by using a place with many visitors (so no one notices them), but the place they choose happens to be the home of a prostitute! Rahab's thoughts and emotions must be mixed. She can't believe they are here. There are only two and they have not come to destroy. Not yet.

She has prepared for this and is ready for what happens next. She knows the king is watching her and it's only a matter of time before someone comes to inquire about her guests. She quickly takes them to her roof where she has been working, where she thought about what she would do if she could meet the people of the one true God. The area is crowded with tools, and most of it is covered in a layer of drying flax stalks she will turn into a profit after she spins it into linen. This is where she instructs them to hide. She returns to the rooms below, waiting for the king's inquiry.

Almost immediately the king's men come knocking on her door.

> Bring out the men who have come to you, who entered your house, for they have come to search out all the land. (Joshua 2:3).

She is brazen in her answer and lies. She risks everything before she has a chance to speak with the two men upstairs. She betrays everyone and everything she knows for the chance to follow something bigger than herself. It's a risk.

> "True, the men came to me, but I did not know where they were from. And when the gate was about to be closed at

dark, the men went out. I do not know where the men went. Pursue them quickly, for you will overtake them." (Joshua 2:4-5)

Sure, it's a risk. But one Rahab is willing to take for the chance to escape destruction.

When she is finally able to talk with the men, she asks for kindness. She begs them to spare her life and the lives of her family members. Being responsible for her parents, siblings, and their families is not new for Rahab. She is a caregiver, a homemaker, a property owner, a business owner and a political insider who cares about those closest to her and wants them to live. In risking her life, she hopes to gain the new life she has always longed for herself and for them.

Too often, we can feel trapped by circumstances and family obligations. We desperately want to trust God to see change, but there is too much at stake. What if our plans backfire? There are too many people counting on us. Who will take care of the future if we don't take care of it ourselves?

But God...

Rahab is given supernatural faith to trust that God would save her family. The two men agree that everyone within the walls of her residence will not be harmed. They keep that promise, and when the city of Jericho is destroyed, the spies go and retrieve "the prostitute"; she and her family are spared (Joshua 6:22-25).

They are saved from destruction, but what now? How does Rahab move forward into this new life? First of all, she doesn't allow the past to define her. She doesn't allow the label, her label, to hold her down because she knows she is more than any label she has ever been given. She is now living with the people of God. She holds her head high. She doesn't look back, only forward. She wins the trust and respect of the people by her actions (Joshua 6:17). And she has faith in a mighty God.

The biggest surprise in the story is how God blesses Rahab in her new life. She becomes the wife of Salmon, one of the spies and a leader in the tribe of Judah. She becomes the mother of Boaz and is the great-great grandmother of King David. She is part of the earthly family of Jesus (Matthew 1:5). Astounding.

God gives each of us second chances for greatness. Not just to escape our circumstances, but to be center stage as part of His plan for us. Rahab is still a prostitute when God uses her. He didn't wait for her circumstances to change before He called her to act. And yet He still credits her faith as righteousness (James 2:25). It's not about who she is or where she's been; it's about who God is and where He is taking her.

God can use anyone in any circumstance to move His plan forward and give Himself glory. God wants to use you. You must have faith and trust Him for who He is in order to move forward.

Soul Activity

God wants to give you the faith you need to believe what He says about you so you can move forward in your business by trusting Him. Today you will be Praying in Color about the word Faith. This will be different because you will use a few verses from Hebrews 11 for your coloring time.

Faith shows the reality of what we hope for; it is the evidence of things we cannot see.

By faith we understand that the entire universe was formed at God's command, that what we now see did not come from anything that can be seen.

And it is impossible to please God without faith. Anyone who wants to come to him must believe that God exists and that he rewards those who sincerely seek him.
(Hebrews 11:1, 3, 6, NLT)

Begin by writing these three verses on your page. You may wish to use one page for each verse. Leave space between the lines and words to be able to mark and color.

First mark the word Faith in a distinctive way. Mark other words that jump out to you (use the same color and/or shape to mark similar concepts). If you wish, you may want to re-write the verses using colors, symbols, or decorative lettering.

As you re-read the verses, make it personal to you. Add thoughts, impressions, words and/or pictures God gives you as you use His Word to discover what He has to say to you about Faith.

Ask God to show you what it means to have the faith to trust Him with your business so you can take risks for Him. Ask Him to grow your faith so you are moving forward in the way He wants for you. Thank Him for who He is and what He has done to give you faith in Him.

Prayer

Lord, You are so good. You have revealed who You are in Your Word. Thank You for giving me all the tools to know and trust You more. Father, I want the kind of faith that has no doubts that You will do a good work in my life. I pray for guidance as I move forward in my business. I pray my faith grows so I take risks for You that change my business. I want to show others my faith in You through my business. In Jesus' name, amen.

Rahab Guided Imagery

This is a guided imagery exercise. Read it through completely before you begin the activity. Refer to the instructions for creating your environment and the breathing exercise in the front of this book to begin relaxing.

After you have relaxed with the breathing, continue to breathe slowly and imagine this scene:

You are standing at the bottom of the wooden steps in Rahab's house. It's a narrow passage that disappears in the curve at the top; these are the steps up to the roof. Place your hand on the cool stone wall as you climb up the stairs. You make the turn at the top and feel the warmth of the sun as you step out on the roof.

As you look around, you see a fabric-covered area in the opposite corner. Set up there is a block of wood with nails sticking out; Rahab uses this to separate and polish the flax fibers. A wooden board with a v-shaped notch at the top is propped up; this is where she stands to smooth the fibers that hang there.

You take a step and your foot catches on the piles of flax stalks covering the space. There's a faint scent of something sweet in the air. You close your eyes and inhale it deeply. This is the place where Rahab made her plan. This was her own place for silence and solitude as she worked. This is where she discovered her faith.

Open your eyes and step through the flax plants. The sun is strong on your face and neck. Move to the edge of the roof to look out, beyond the thick city wall. Shield your eyes from the sun and take a look over the countryside. The rolling hills are magnificent against the sky.

You turn back and walk carefully to the working corner of the roof. The makeshift tent flutters in the breeze. There is a low stool in the shade and you make your way to sit. What plans do you need to make? What action is next for you? Sit here in silence on the roof and wait for God to speak to your heart. Ask Him for faith to move forward. Stretch out your legs and rest. Listen to what God wants to tell you.

Lie there as long as you wish until you are ready to move. Continue breathing deeply until you want to get up and reflect.

Response Activity

Once you have completed the imagery exercise, use your journal or a piece of paper to reflect on what God revealed to you about the plans and actions you need to make to move forward in your business. What change does He want you to make? Record the feelings and thoughts you experienced as you sat and listened to what He had to say to your heart. Express joy and gratitude for the faith He has given you.

Prayer

Father, WOW! You have given me hope! Thank You for who You are. Thank You for Your gift of salvation. Lord, You amaze me over and over again with how You work in the lives of Your people. Just as You gave Rahab a second chance and a new beginning, I pray for a chance to change, too. I trust You to give me the strength to make that change because I cannot do it alone. I know I can only move forward if I have faith in who You are and not in who I am. Help me grow in my faith. In Jesus' name, amen.

Mind Activity

Principle: **My business moves forward because I trust God for who He is.**

God gave you the vision for your business. Only you can accomplish the mission of your life. God gives supernatural gifts so you can live out His calling on your life. Are you confident in His plan and His provision for every decision you make?

Rahab's spiritual gift of faith gave her the ability to believe God would do things that were impossible for her apart from His involvement. Do you have faith that God can work the seemingly impossible in your life? What spiritual gifts is God infusing into you so you can trust Him to move forward in your business?

Rahab's actions were courageous and she was given supernatural faith to stand on the side of God's people. Using faith in your business means you are looking to God to do big things. Trust God to give you exactly what you need, when you need it, to do exactly what He wants you to do to move forward and work in your business.

The goal for this principle is best formulated by knowing your spiritual gifts. There are many assessments you can take to discover yours. Your goal needs to include the action (how to apply it) you will take in your business based on your gift(s).

Write out your Goal.

S
M
A
R
T

Here is an example using one of my spiritual gifts: I will use my gift of teaching to create a workshop in two months on using LinkedIn for connecting with your ideal clients. It will be set up for ten participants. This workshop will establish my expertise with social media.

Strength Activity

Principle: **My business moves forward because I trust God for who He is.**

Give God everything. In order to use your spiritual gifts in your business, you must first surrender them to God for His use. He has so much to give you if you are willing to give it back to Him and use it the way He desires.

Once you have taken an assessment and know your top three to six spiritual gifts, begin with prayer. Take your journal and place each word at the top of a page and ask God how He wants you to use it in your business.

Brainstorm, bullet, or draw the ideas He gives you.

Look at all aspects of your business and decide how each part of your business will look when you add your spiritual gifts to each area. Write out the day-to-day actions you can take to demonstrate that gift. Ask God to bless your use of His super-imposed gift to you to help your business move forward. Trust God with the result.

Write out your action steps for this goal.

Prayer

Lord, I do trust You and want to be used by You in my business. Just like Rahab, I pray for the faith to know You are working things out for me to move forward. Thank You for giving me the spiritual gifts I have and help me to use them in my business to show You to others. Father, I pray for Your guidance as I seek to do Your will and represent You in the marketplace. Help me to keep trusting You for the results in my business. In Jesus' name, amen.

9

Huldah:
Building a Strong
Reputation

Read the Biblical account of Huldah in 2 Kings 22:8-20 and 2 Chronicles 34:14-33.

Principle: **The choices I make build my reputation in the marketplace.**

Choosing to Do the Work

When we meet Huldah, we immediately know she is an intelligent, straight-forward, respected woman in her community. Huldah is part of the Jewish elite in Jerusalem. She sits in the "college" of the temple, advising others and interpreting God's Word; she is a prophetess. Huldah also has a school for women, teaching God's call for Jewish mothers and daughters.

Huldah's husband, Shallum, holds a prominent position in the royal court as the keeper of the royal wardrobe for all occasions. This gives him daily access to the king, and we can suppose it gives Huldah access to the queen. They are known instructors and confidants to the royal family. As Huldah helps Queen Jedidah with her outfits each day, she uses her time wisely by giving counsel about royal affairs while assisting her.

Jewish literature says Queen Jedidah was a godly woman because when King Josiah takes the throne at the age of eight, he has been influenced greatly by his mother. As the Queen's "dresser," Huldah surely also has opportunities to share knowledge and teach not only the queen, but the young prince. In a time when no one knows God's Law, this leaves a lasting impression on Josiah.

Building a reputation takes time. Huldah has spent her entire life in the pursuit of knowledge; she loves learning and God has rewarded her with the gift of discernment. Huldah is not famous, but she is known. During this time in Jewish history, the temple is destroyed and the Jews are worshipping other gods. Her sphere of influence is limited because of this disarray. Life is full of turmoil for the Jewish nation and there is no stability.

Our own world today is the same. Everyone is doing their own thing and there seems to be no moral authority. We can feel like it doesn't matter what we do or how we act, like nobody's paying attention. But someone is always watching our behavior, our reactions to situations, and how we respond to others. Huldah is being watched and so are you.

Statistics say it takes ten years of focused study to become an expert in any field. Huldah has put in the time to establish her expertise. I think she got started by hearing the stories of Deborah and imagining herself in the heroic adventures. This excitement draws her to study the Scriptures. But Huldah knows Deborah (who comes later in this book) is an exception, and does not expect God to use her in such a big way. She is content to follow her passion and learn more about God's Word.

Are you following your passion or do you feel like you're just treading water, just putting in time? Putting in time isn't always a bad thing; Huldah gains respect and recognition by putting in her time and not expecting big results. She develops her experience with no expectations of a promotion. We are different from Huldah in that way: we have opportunities for advancement if we gain more knowledge, but she has already hit her glass ceiling. She probably knows more and is more qualified to teach the Torah than those in authority over her, but she can do nothing about it.

Yet she chooses to work hard. She is giving her best right where she is and God blesses her for it. Her expertise and experience have primed her for what will happen next. She is ready when God calls.

Heart Activity

Reflection Questions:

How have you built expertise and experience in your work?

What actions are shaping your reputation in the marketplace?

How will you build the reputation you want in your business?

Prayer

Father, I come before You with a deep appreciation for the talents and gifts You have given me. I thank You for my mind and for the opportunities to learn and grow in my profession. Lord, You have given me the strength and stamina to keep working and achieving even when it is hard. Help me work with distinction in my business environment. Help me develop a reputation of excellence that brings You glory. In Jesus' name, amen.

Choosing to Do the Work Well

Fast forward almost two decades. Huldah's day comes eighteen years after Josiah has become king. He is still under 30 and Huldah is much older and wiser. Since he was sixteen, Josiah has been a wonderful king and has implemented many spiritual practices previously lost in the nation of Israel. I am sure Huldah has had many opportunities to teach and guide eager students in this newfound enthusiasm for God. Her reputation has grown as more and more Jews return to learn God's Law.

There is a huge project going on in Jerusalem now: King Josiah has commissioned the restoration of the temple. It's in shambles and needs lots of TLC. In the clean up, the high priest, Hilkiah, discovers a lost scroll. It's actually an original manuscript of Deuteronomy penned by Moses—it had been lost in a mess of rubble and trash!

Hilkiah sends it to Josiah, and when it's read to him he tears his clothes in anguish over its words. He sends the priests back to the temple to inquire of the Lord on his behalf because he realized God was angry with His people. The priests go to Huldah for counsel. They may have thought she was going to give the king a more compassionate and tender meaning to the judgment described in the scroll because she was a woman. But we know Huldah's reputation is one of being direct and truthful about God's Word; she has a gift for interpreting it.

Huldah is not afraid to exercise her authority and gets to the point. She first authenticates the book: it is indeed part of the Law. Her years of study and experience have taught her to recognize

God's Word. She is clear in the task; she does not try to make herself look more important, but works at the job she is asked to do. Too often, we choose to do the work we want to do instead of the work in front of us. We must earn respect and a good reputation by doing the job given to us; only then can we move up.

But Huldah then takes her job a step farther. She gives more than is expected—unlimited by her job description, she becomes indispensable. God gives her a prophecy:

> "This is what the LORD says: I am going to bring disaster on this city and its people. All the words written in the scroll that the king of Judah has read will come true. For my people have abandoned me and offered sacrifices to pagan gods, and I am very angry with them for everything they have done. My anger will burn against this place, and it will not be quenched." (2 Kings 22:15-17 NLT)

Huldah doesn't have a pleasant message to deliver, but she doesn't back down from delivering it. And she does have words of encouragement for Josiah: She tells him this destruction would not take place in his lifetime because of his humble and honest reaction to the words in the scroll.

There is an immediate call to repent and turn back to God, and the whole Jewish nation renews their covenant. Huldah's prophecy and influence causes a great spiritual revival in the Jewish people. Her quiet strength is easy to overlook, but she has an important role to play and serves her people when they need it.

Most of us, like Huldah, will never be famous for our exploits. But we can easily model her path and build solid reputations by pursuing excellence, gaining expertise, and attaining more experience. It may take more time than we want, but our job is to keep focused on the work in front of us, what God is calling us to do right now. There is no fast lane in building a good reputation. It's in the choices you make every day: the things you do to go beyond the expectations of your customers, clients, colleagues, and co-workers that build the reputation you want—and the one God wants for you.

Soul Activity

Before you go to prayer today, brainstorm words that come to mind when you think about someone with a good reputation. These attributes might be integrity, loyal, intelligence, stability, honesty, reliable, sincere, etc. Write the words you think of at the top of your journal page or paper.

Today you will be Praying in Color about your own reputation in the marketplace. At the center of your page, write your own name. Draw a bubble, cloud, or shape around it. Color and doodle on the page. Use the words you brainstormed at the top of your page and incorporate the attributes you are aspiring to demonstrate in your reputation. Write them in shapes around your name or connect them with lines.

Add colors, lines, marks and shapes. Ask God to show you what actions you need to establish to grow in these areas so your reputation increases. Draw the images and/or write the words He impresses on you.

Ask God if there are any other attributes He wants you to incorporate into your reputation, and include those in your drawing as well.

Prayer

Lord, You are amazing. You say in Your Word that You wish for me to grow in excellence (1 Peter 1:3-8) so I can be more productive for You. Father, You have shown me that by developing a good reputation, I honor You. I know that only by connecting with You each day will I be able to do that. Help me work with excellence and make choices each day that reflect the attributes and characteristics You have shown me. Transform me little by little every day to be more like Your Son. In Jesus' name, amen.

Huldah Guided Imagery

This is a guided imagery exercise. Read it through completely before you begin the activity. Refer to the instructions for creating your environment and the breathing exercise in the front of this book to begin relaxing.

After you have relaxed with the breathing exercises, continue to breathe slowly and imagine this scene:

You are standing on the wide steps of a three-story stone building. The grey rock glistens in the sunlight from a thousand flecks of quartz embedded in it. You climb the low risers to the revolving door and enter a large, open room. You look out and see the light streaming in through the floor-to-ceiling windows at the opposite end of this huge expanse.

Your eyes move to the area at the center of the room. There are two rows of long mahogany tables with curving chairs and individual green glass lights. It is a study library.

You look up and your eye follows the balconies of shelves lined with books. There is a hum of low conversation reverberating off the marble floor. To your right, you hear a ding and you look to see the elevator has just arrived. Two young adults with backpacks are looking over a book as they exit and talk quietly.

You pass them and enter the elevator. You press the third-floor button and feel the elevator's slight jump as it lets go of the floor and lifts. When the doors open, you step out onto a carpeted floor. It is soft, and muffles the sounds around you.

You cross the short distance to look down onto the big area where students of all ages are sitting and studying. It's a long way down, and you feel a little dizzy from the height.

You move back from the edge and turn to the rows of books behind you. Slowly, you move between the volumes, weaving in and out of the short rows. You run your hand along the books and your fingers bump along their spines. The smell of paper and glue is familiar to you, and it takes you back to your years spent in the library—the years of studying, learning, growing your expertise.

You stop and pull a book from the shelf; it is one you know. It is one that gave you inspiration when you decided to do what you are doing now. You hold it in your hands and smile, remembering. You take it over to a small cubby desk set up at the outside of the balcony. You lay it open and smooth the pages with your hands.

You look toward the windows and think about the journey you have taken, the choices you have made to get to where you are today. God's presence comes over you right there in the small booth, and you express gratitude to Him for His guidance in your life. You ask Him to show you the way to keep building your reputation through your daily choices and actions. You thank Him for allowing you to represent Him through your business. You close your eyes and lean back in the hard seat, sitting quietly as God speaks to your heart about your next steps.

Lie there as long as you wish until you are ready to move. Continue breathing deeply until you want to get up and reflect.

Response Activity

Once you have completed the imagery exercise, use your journal or a piece of paper to reflect on what God revealed to you about the actions to take and the choices to make in order to build a solid reputation in the marketplace. Be sure to record the feelings and thoughts you experienced as you walked through and sat in the library.

Prayer

God, thank You for the incredible story of Huldah. Thank You for meeting me wherever I am and speaking to my heart. I love how You guide me in all areas of my life. You have given me the expertise I need to do my job well and You direct my actions each day so I continue to develop a good reputation in my marketplace. Help me be the person You have called me to be. Guide me to make wise decisions to grow my reputation and show Your goodness to others. In Jesus' name, amen.

Mind Activity

Principle: **The choices I make build my reputation in the marketplace.**

Statistics say it takes ten years of focused study to become an expert in any field, and building a reputation can take just as long. That is not meant to discourage you; it is meant to encourage you to keep going. God only requires you to take the next step, trust Him, and do what is in front of you.

How do you want to show up in your marketplace? How does God want you to showcase your expertise?

Are you in a place of preparation right now? Embrace it and create a goal that gives you motivation to persevere.

Are you moving ahead in your passion and deciding how you want to show up in your marketplace? Take time to talk with God about which character qualities He wants you to focus on to build your reputation.

Creating a goal in this area will take daily effort. Forming a habit is important so you achieve and maintain this goal. Pray and think about three attributes you can incorporate into your daily routine that will grow your reputation and position you to be seen as an expert.

Write out your Goal.

S

M

A

R

T

My goal for this principle consists of the three attributes I want to grow my reputation around: to be authentic so I can lead more openly, continue learning so others always know I am the one with the information, and to be reliable so others can count on me.

Based on this brainstorm, an example of a SMART goal is: I will lead my networking group with authenticity by sharing personal struggles I am having in my business. By sharing in the group I am able to get input from my members for possible solutions. This will create trust and others will know I am real.

Strength Activity

Principle: **The choices I make build my reputation in the marketplace.**

Once you have decided on the three character qualities, deconstruct them into actionable steps you can do to build your reputation in that area. After you have established these three characteristics, you can continue adding others with the same pattern.

I deconstructed the above goal by deciding what activities would help me live out these qualities. By creating habits, the actions become automatic. Creating a habit takes three things: reminder, routine, and reward.

If you start with the reward, it will keep you motivated to set up the reminder and to do the routine. What is your reward for displaying the character quality you chose? Mine is that I like being seen as the go-to person. One of my strengths is Significance, and I want to work in my strengths.

Reminders can be:

Timers
Blocks in your calendar
Physical objects
Actions

When the reminder is triggered, you do the routine—the actual behavior you decided on to create the habit. It is not dependent on you feeling like doing the behavior; just do it. For my continued learning quality, I have created the habit of listening to books on CD while in my car and I listen to podcasts while doing my hair and makeup each morning. These habits keep my learning quality a reputation-building strategy.

Now it's time to add your action plan and create a habit to incorporate into your lifestyle.

Prayer

Lord, You are so good to me. I thank You for these tools that help me lead a disciplined life. I pray that the character qualities You are growing in me inspire others. I pray I can be Your representative in the marketplace by creating a reputation that honors You. Thank You for allowing me to serve You in this way. In Jesus' name, amen.

10

Ruth:
Devoted to the Work

Read the Biblical account of Ruth in the book of the Bible named for her.

Principle: **My devotion to God gives me the strength to be consistent in my business.**

Work is Necessary

The first thing evident about Ruth is that she is a loyal and devoted daughter-in-law. Naomi and her family came to Moab because there was a famine in Judah; they were looking for a better place for the family. Naomi's two sons marry Moabite women after their father dies, and while that wasn't forbidden, it was highly frowned upon. (The Moabites are Lot's descendants.) But then both the sons die, leaving Ruth and Orpah as childless widows—just like Naomi.

They have been family for ten years when Naomi hears a report that the famine is over. She wants to return to Bethlehem. She has become a bitter old woman (and she knows it) but knows her people, the Jews, care for their widows; she will do much better at home. She urges her daughters-in-law to go home and find new husbands who can give them a better life. Orpah, though sad, does return to her parents. Ruth, however, refuses. She has a different plan.

Life sometimes does not happen the way we plan. I am laughing as I write that! It is true—we have our perfect plans for how life is going to unfold. I can look back and say my life did not always go in the direction I planned, but I see it happened just the way God planned. You may be on a branch of your path right now, not quite on the path you thought you would be on. God does that at times to see how you step into the situation so He can grow your character.

Maybe Ruth saw no hope in her own homeland for a decent husband, but I have to think after ten years with Naomi she has come to believe in the one true God. When Naomi tries to dissuade her for a second time, she pleads with her and says she will go wherever Naomi goes and she will worship the God Naomi worships (Ruth 1:16). Ruth is determined to not let go of Naomi and is totally devoted to her. That shows us Ruth's character as a woman ready to do whatever is necessary to help her mother-in-law and be the woman God is calling her to be.

When they arrive in Bethlehem, many are pleased Naomi is back. She apparently has a lively reputation. But she quickly makes it known she is a broken, bitter woman. And the foreign woman Naomi brought back—Ruth—is also the subject of much talk.

Ruth knows unless they find a source of income, or at least a source of food, they will die. Having been taught well by Naomi, she knows she can gather the extra grain from the fields because that is the way of the Israelites. Ruth is smart and adopts their ways quickly. She asks Naomi's permission to go to the fields to find food. Ruth ends up in fields belonging to Boaz, Naomi's relative.

God orchestrated everything so Ruth would be safe and not suffer. She discovers quickly her "luck" and now, if someone asks, she cab tell them the connection, if there is any dispute as to why she is there.

They have arrived at the beginning of spring harvest. Ruth begins working in the fields, gleaning the leftover grain to feed Naomi and herself. This type of work is back-breaking as she trails behind the paid harvesters to collect anything that remains. She is probably not the only gleaner in the crowd, either. This mandate from God—to leave certain parts of fields unharvested—was to help widows, orphans, and foreigners. And it extends to Ruth on all levels. The work may not be what she wanted, it may be beneath her pay grade, but it's what is in front of her so she and Naomi can survive.

The work is hard and long, but we don't see Ruth complaining or grumbling. In fact, she works hard every day, picking up the leftovers from the field. This situation is fraught with dangers from the paid harvesters (men) and the other gleaners as well. To be a woman in this environment has got to be difficult.

Have you ever had a job where you were just going through the motions? Just trying to make it through each day to get your paycheck? God calls us to more. He calls us to pursue excellence. Ruth is doing just that as she gleans in the fields. She is our example of showing a good attitude and doing our best.

Eventually, Boaz notices the beautiful woman working in the field and asks about her. The foreman reports she has a strong work ethic, and this finds favor with Boaz. He is an encouraging boss and tells her to glean only from his fields, to go behind the women for safety, and to get all the water she needs. He even instructs the harvesters to give her extra food at lunch and to drop extra grain for her to pick up. This reward is for going beyond what is expected for her mother-in-law.

Ruth shows us that hard work sets us apart.

Heart Activity

Reflection Questions:

Have you ever been as devoted to something or someone as Ruth is to Naomi? What was it and why were you so committed?

What has been your attitude when you've had to do a job that wasn't exactly using your level of expertise?

How does pursuing excellence in your work reflect your devotion to God?

Describe a time when you worked hard and were rewarded in some way.

Prayer

Father, thank You for opportunities to show my devotion to You. Thank You for Your presence in my everyday life. Please keep my attitudes be positive each day as I labor in my present work. Help me pursue excellence right where you have me. Help me continue to be shaped by You and to be more like You in both my actions and attitudes. I trust You to use my present circumstances to bring me into the future You have for me. In Jesus' name, amen.

Work Brings Reward

From the first day of Ruth working in Boaz's field, she is a beacon of hope to Naomi. The day she came home with more than enough food for the two of them, talking about where she had been gleaning, Naomi's heart began to soften.

She knew Boaz could save them both.

Ruth stays through the entire harvest, working diligently in Boaz's fields. The barley and wheat harvest together constituted about seven weeks' worth of work. In all this time, Ruth's only concern is to take care of Naomi. Now, Ruth is intelligent, strong, and loyal to a fault; I'm sure she was planning for the next thing after the harvest. I don't know if she had the same thought as Naomi, but Naomi's shrewd, courageous, and persevering nature was reawakened at the thought of Ruth finding favor with Boaz.

The next thing Naomi instructs Ruth to do is daring and risky. It's the time of the threshing. Boaz and his men will be staying at the barn for some male camaraderie and to protect the grain. Naomi sees the perfect opportunity to save Ruth and herself. Since Boaz is a relative, she wants Ruth to appeal to his kinsman-redeemer obligation. That is, ask him to marry her.

What's risky about that? Well, first she has to be bold enough to go to him, and there's a good chance she'll be rejected and labeled a whore. But Ruth's devotion to her mother-in-law is steadfast. She does exactly as she is told and prepares herself to go to Boaz and ceremonially uncover his feet while he sleeps. Then she'll ask for him to cover her with his garment and solidify his commitment to her.

Imagine being that far out of your comfort zone! Doing something you know is the right thing but being totally scared to do it. I think Ruth saw this as a great opportunity to help Naomi and herself, but it took real courage to move forward with the plan. We each have moments like this in our businesses; we seize scary and sometimes risky opportunities to move forward. But these are necessary so we learn to trust God at every stage.

Happily, Boaz does identify Ruth as a woman worthy of his attention. Ruth may seem like an unimportant person who is just looking to survive, but God has other plans. Boaz accepts Ruth and she is given the great privilege of having children as well. In fact, she is the mother of Obed, the grandfather of King David. She's in the lineage of Jesus!

We can never overlook the importance of our work by the size of our bank accounts, our popularity in the market, or position at the company. God sees your heart and is shaping your character to be more like His. God is using you to shape the future.

If we did not have this hope, we would be sad about having to eke out a living, expecting nothing to come from it. But we do have God behind our work. He is giving us the power each day to get up and go. We do not depend on our own ability to make it happen; we depend on the God we serve to make it all work out for our benefit.

Your job is to work faithfully and know the work you are doing right now is where you need to be to move into what God will ask you to do next.

Soul Activity

Ruth accepted the position she was in and worked diligently. God is asking you to work where He has placed you. Today you will be Praying in Color about your present work and your attitude toward it. You will also be looking to where God wants to move you next.

Create two spaces in your journal for the words Present and Future. (You may want to use two pages or place them side by side on one page.)

Start with the word Present. Draw a bubble, cloud, or shape around the word. Use lines, drawings, and colors to think about your attitude toward the work you are doing. Ask God to show you how He is using this present work to shape your character and make you more like Him. Add words to the drawing as they come. Discover where God has you and for what purpose.

Next, move on to the word Future. Thank God for having a purpose in your work now and connect it to where He wants to take you next. What is that thought in your heart you know can only be coming from God? What is the dream saying in that small, quiet voice inside you? Write it out here and allow God to show you His heart. Continue to color and doodle on the page. Ask God to show you the next step He has for you. Thank Him for shaping you into the person He wants you to be.

Add other colors, lines, marks, and shapes. Ask God for wisdom to keep moving in the direction He wants you to go. Draw the images and write the words He impresses on your heart as He reveals your next steps in the marketplace.

Prayer

Father, thank You for the life of Ruth. She shows me I, too, can be Your example right where I am in my present work. I know You want me to be transformed into Your image. Thank You for working on me each day. Help me be patient with this process. Give me hope that the future will be exactly what You have for me and that it will be good. Help me trust You for creating a future that will excite and be good for me. Thank You for guiding me through the steps You want me to take. In Jesus' name, amen.

Ruth Guided Imagery

This is a guided imagery exercise. Read it through completely before you begin the activity. Refer to the instructions for creating your environment and the breathing exercise in the front of this book to begin relaxing.

After you have relaxed with the breathing, continue to breathe slowly and imagine this scene:

Go to your garden. It may be the planter in the front of your house, a vegetable garden in the backyard, or some potted plants on your porch or deck. Imagine it's spring. The air is crisp in the warm sunshine, winter's last hurrah.

You are planting today. This may not be something you do often, but today feels right and you want to see the fruit of your labor this summer. Collect all your tools: cart, spade, rake, fertilized dirt, flowers, or vegetables. Put on your hat and gloves and place all the other items in your cart.

Move into your garden area. Watch as a bird flies by and see where it lands on the tree above. Listen to its message as it also welcomes spring. Breathe in the fresh air and smell the damp earth.

Get to work clearing the area of last year's weeds. Feel the strain of your muscles as you clear it out. See the fresh new ground ready for your new plants. One by one, line up the new plants where they are going to be placed.

Kneel in the soft dirt and turn over the soil with your hands. The cold, wet soil seeps through your gloves and you welcome the opportunity to do manual work. Smile as you visualize what they will look like when they fill in the space. Thank God for His renewal. Thank Him for reminding you that He will bless what you plant.

Dig holes for each of your plants and place them in the spaces. Throw in the good soil to help with their growth. Gently pat the soil around each and secure them into place. Think about how satisfying this is to be here, on your knees, working the ground.

Feel the earth under your knees and legs. Feel the security of God holding you up at this moment. This may not be your normal work, but you feel satisfied in it at this moment. Feel the humility of being before God. Ask Him to bless your present work. Ask Him to create a vision for the future work He has for you. Thank Him for the satisfaction of doing the work you have now.

Imagine, as you kneel here on His creation, that He is beside you. Feel His presence ever so slightly on your leg and arm. Tell Him aloud the things you are grateful for. Thank Him specifically for how He is shaping you into His image. Lean into His side as He puts His arm around you. Feel His strength flow into you. Breathe in the warmth of His body next to yours. Stay embraced and hear what He wants to say to you.

Lie there as long as you wish until you are ready to move. Continue breathing deeply until you want to get up and reflect.

Response Activity

Once you have completed the imagery exercise, use your journal or a piece of paper to reflect on what God revealed to you about your present work and where He wants to take you. What is it like to spend time just being with Him in His creation? Be sure to record the feelings and thoughts you experienced as you worked in your garden and humbled yourself before God.

Prayer

God, thank You for the things You have spoken to me in my garden. Remind me to meet with You each day as I humble myself before You. Let me be satisfied with the work You have given me and help me remember it is all for my good. I thank You for shaping me into the exact person You want me to be. Help me trust You as I learn more about You. I pray to deepen my relationship with You so I can grow in my faith. Help me show You in the work You have me doing now and in the future. In Jesus' name, amen.

Mind Activity

Principle: **My devotion to God gives me strength to be consistent in my business.**

Ruth's total dependence on God is shown through her actions. Like her, we do not depend on our own ability to make it happen. We depend on the God we serve to make it all work out for our benefit. Your job is to work faithfully, pursuing excellence; know the work you are doing right now is where you need to be to move into what God will ask you to do next.

The goal for this principle demonstrates your consistency in showing up with excellence in your work. Consistency does three things for you: it allows you to measure if something is working, it creates accountability, and it makes you relevant. How can you show up in your work more consistently?

When you are working in your values—those things or ideas that are most important to you—it is easy to stay consistent and be authentic. Take the time each day to be mindful of the present moment and appreciate what you are doing in that moment no matter the task. Your goal for this principle should reflect how you are going to be consistent in showing up with excellence in your work.

Write out your Goal.

S

M

A

R

T

Here is an example: To show up consistently in my writing, I will write 1,000 words per day. I will schedule a two-hour time block in my day so I create the content I need for my book.

Strength Activity

Principle: **My devotion to God gives me strength to be consistent in my business.**

Consistency-in-action is about gaining ever greater insights and understandings about what you are doing, and then making the necessary adjustments to these actions to help improve your results and performance over time.

To be consistent means understanding the greatest power lies in the present moment. Therefore, consistency demands that you stay mindful and present on the task at hand without losing focus. It demands you to discipline yourself to this moment, and only to this moment without exception.

Get very clear about what your highest-priority activities are. These activities are typically built around your values and purpose. You will only stay consistent in your business if you know these.

Once you are clear about the priorities you will focus on, it's now time to develop a schedule that will help you to block out specific time throughout the day when you will spend time working on these highest-priority activities. Remember to focus on what's most important, not what's fun, easy, or convenient. Focus on one thing at a time, not on trying to multi-task (your brain cannot do it.). Lastly, focus on the completion of an activity, not on the desired outcome. It takes perseverance before you see results.

Write your action plan.

Prayer

Lord, thank You for my ability to be mindful and stay focused on the tasks that will move my business forward. Help me depend on You for the stamina to stay consistent and show up each day ready to work. Please give me a positive attitude as I work to do the activities that really matter. Father, guide me to know where to put my energy. Help me persevere and leave the results to You. In Jesus' name, amen.

11

Deborah:
Be a Leader

Read the Biblical account of Deborah in Judges 4-5.

Principle: **God expects me to be a leader in the marketplace.**

Your Position as a Leader

Deborah is a leader among her people—a judge and a prophet. No other person during the time of the judges has this distinction. In fact, she is considered one of Israel's best judges. Her job is that of a political leader as well as a spiritual leader. Her office is under a date palm tree that sits in the hill country of Ephraim. The entire nation comes to her for counsel (Judges 4:5)!

Deborah is a wife and probably a mother, too. Since she is well-respected, prestigious, and has a lot of responsibility outside the home, she has had to decide which jobs to delegate. It looks as though her household is taken care of by either her husband, Lappidoth (the first stay-at-home dad?), or someone else. This frees her to operate squarely in her role of political and spiritual leader as a judge.

Taking your business to the professional level requires you to give up other roles you think belong to you: cleaning, grocery shopping, creating meals, laundry, social media marketing, accounting, etc. Unless one of these activities IS your business, I think it's safe to say you can delegate them to someone else. Deborah knows what she is good at and she puts all of her time and energy into that, not other things that can be delegated.

Deborah is a leader; God has called her to this position and she takes it seriously. Imagine sitting in the shade of the palm tree giving advice and dispensing justice to the entire nation of Israel and then receiving a message from God.

The Israelites have been oppressed by the Canaanites for 20 years. They are controlled through force by the commander, Sisera, and his 900 chariots. After such a long time, the people cry out to God for relief (Judges 4:3) and Deborah gets the message! God gives the answer to the Israelites' problem through a woman.

The message from God is for Barak. He has been chosen by God to lead the forces against Sisera. She instructs him to assemble 10,000 men to fight Sisera's army (Judges 4:6). She tells Barak how she will lure Sisera to a section along the Kishon River so they will have the advantage. Then something even more surprising happens: Barak refuses to go into battle unless she goes with him. Deborah is quick in her response to his request. She says she will gladly go with him, but because of his cowardice, he will not get the glory for the defeat; it will go to the hands of a woman. And she has to be wondering if she would be the one to kill Sisera.

Not only does Deborah receive the prophecy from God as the spiritual leader, she now becomes the commander-in-chief of the armed forces.

Do you see her leadership? She is decisive when Barak refuses to go into battle without her. She shows confidence in her prophecy by telling him he will not get any credit for Sisera's death. She displays inspiration and focus as she reveals the plan and gives God credit for its success.

You are a leader, too.

Each day there are many decisions you must make for the success of your business and family. No matter if you're leading ten or 10,000, you display confidence—you inspire—and you focus on the task at hand. God will give you what you need to succeed just as He did for Deborah.

Heart Activity

Reflection Questions:

Have you ever received a message from God specifically regarding your business? What happened?

What tasks or activities in your household or business have you delegated to someone else? How does that feel for you?

Deborah is doing what she is best at. If you were able to do only the thing you're best at in your business, what would it be?

In what ways are you leading your business?

Prayer

Lord, thank You for Your direct messages and downloads into my business. As I work to do my best each day, I pray I would hear from You the way Deborah did. I pray for help to do my best and be the leader You have called me to be. Father, I want my business to be professional and I trust You will make it exactly what You desire. Help me be faithful to Your vision for my business. In Jesus' name, amen.

Trusting God to Help You Lead

Barak does as Deborah instructs and begins assembling the 10,000-man army from the tribes of Naphtali and Zebulun. Sisera gets word the Israelites are organizing on Mount Tabor and positions himself exactly where Deborah says he would be for his defeat. Incredible.

"Get ready! This is the day the Lord will give you victory over Sisera, for the Lord is marching ahead of you," Deborah says to Barak (Judges 4:14, NLT). She always puts herself behind God, always willing to allow God to take the first place. She knew she needed God's help to do the job He had given her. She doesn't back down from the new role as military leader; she embraces God's message and moves ahead bravely.

Many times you may feel unqualified for the task in front of you. God is always stretching us to make us more like Him. It can be scary. I am sure Deborah was scared; undoubtedly, adrenaline coursed through her body that day. You can use your adrenaline to move through the scary moments. It can give you courage to take the next step right now.

What an inspiration Deborah is to Barak and his men. She announces their victory before they have even begun. They charge down the mountain toward the river basin, toward Sisera's 900 chariots and armed men. God then does something unexpected: He causes all Sisera's men and chariots to panic in a way not typical of their position. The fighting is fierce and Sisera jumps from his chariot to escape on foot.

He runs far enough from the battle that he finds himself in the tents of those who assist Canaanite King Jabin's armies (a.k.a., Sisera). In fact, he runs right to Jael's tent. Jael's husband, Heber, is a Kenite. They are metal workers and follow the Canaanite troops to find work by repairing weapons and chariots.

She is a Bedouin, not an Israelite. But she appears to be more loyal to them than to the Canaanites her husband serves. She invites Sisera into the tent for protection and puts him under a cover to hide him. Since the customs of the time only allow the husband and father of a women to enter their tent, Sisera knows this is an ideal hiding place. He asks her for water but instead, she strategically gives him goat's milk so he is lulled into a false sense of security. He falls asleep after he tells her to keep watch.

We know Deborah's words, and so does Barak—the victory for today would go to a woman. But does Jael know? The battle is still raging down along the river bank; Barak's men are pushing them downstream and everyone in Sisera's army is dying (Judges 14:16). All the while, Sisera is asleep in the tent of an ally.

Jael is compelled to help the Israelites, though she has no allegiance to them. She makes a decision. We are not told what was going through her mind, but her actions are definitely celebrated when Deborah recalls the events of the day in song (Judges 5). As Sisera sleeps, exhausted from the day's battle, Jael drives a tent spike through his temple and kills him. Yuck!

How can she do this? I can just feel her heart pounding as she lures him into the tent, planning exactly what she is going to do. She chooses the tent spike because it is what she knows how to use. As a Bedouin woman, she is responsible for pitching and striking the tent, the home. She knows how to drive stakes into the ground!

Jael stands in contrast to Deborah. Jael, not an Israelite and probably not a believer in God, simply uses what she knows best to complete the task in front of her; Deborah needs to depend on God for her leadership position that day because leading an army is not in her experience like Jael's stake-pounding is. Leadership takes risk and courage; both women showed that, but true leadership takes trust in God. Deborah trusts that what God had said would come to pass.

You also must look beyond what you are capable of doing and see what God is calling you to do. Leading others takes dependence on God. Use your leadership skills and dependence on God to set your business apart in your industry. Be a leader others can aspire to.

Soul Activity

Before you pray today, brainstorm words that come to mind when you think about leadership. Think about qualities of a leader or what you think makes a good leader. Write the brainstormed words at the top of your journal page or paper.

Today you will be Praying in Color about your own qualities as a business leader. At the center of your page, write your own name and draw a bubble, cloud, or shape around it. Continue to color and doodle on the page. Use the words you brainstormed at the top of your page and incorporate the qualities you are aspiring to demonstrate as a leader in your business. Get creative; write them in shapes around your name or connect them with lines.

As you keep doodling, ask God to show you what actions or habits you need to establish to develop these areas so your leadership skills can grow. Draw the images and/or write the words He impresses on you.

Ask God if there are any other qualities He wants you to build into your leadership style. Write any new words and/or actions He gives you.

Prayer

Lord, thank You for showing me You expect me to be a leader right where I am. I accept this responsibility and pray to grow in this area. I want to lead others through my business. Thank You for the opportunity to inspire others to live for You by leading them through my business. Help me each day. In Jesus' name, amen.

Deborah Guided Imagery

This is a guided imagery exercise. Read it through completely before you begin the activity. Refer to the instructions for creating your environment and the breathing exercise in the front of this book to begin relaxing.

After you have relaxed with the breathing, continue to breathe slowly and imagine this scene:

You are sitting under Deborah's palm tree. A warm breeze sweeps across your face as you sit in the shade of the palm. There are several palms here creating a large shady patch. Feel the ground under your body, dry and hard, but comfortably so. Relax your weight onto the ground and enjoy the quiet.

Take a big breath in through your nose and smell the sweet aroma of the dates. More than a flower smell, it almost seems like a tangy candy treat. This is where you work. Day-in and day-out people come to you for advice and help with settling disputes. And you're good at it.

Thank God for such a beautiful place to work! Thank Him for giving you a business that uses your unique gifts and abilities.

Watch as a small group approaches you, sits before you, and begins presenting their case to you. But you are engrossed in the beauty of the moment. If this was your job you would be listening, asking for more information, and making decisions. But it is not your world.

Remember the feeling under the palm tree and imagine yourself now in your office, wherever that may be. It could be your sofa, your kitchen table, or your desk. Maybe it's an actual office in your home or in a building. Place yourself in your workspace and bring the palm tree office feeling into the space.

Look around at where you sit each day to lead your business. Find things in the space that remind you of the things you love. See your organization system and smile at how clean or messy it is. If you begin to feel anxious about the area, tighten your muscles and then relax again. Allow yourself to feel the emotion of your office.

Now imagine what would make the space best for you. What would the office, table, or desk look like to make it your best space to listen to clients, make decisions, and lead through your business? Begin readjusting the space to make it ideal. Place the organization systems where they would work best for you, add favorite mementos so the space becomes special, position the chair to give you the view you want, change anything to make the area your date palm office.

Look at what you have created. Invite Jesus to see your space. Ask Him to sit down and look around. Smile at what you have accomplished to create a space you love. See Him looking at you and smiling. His face shows how proud He is of you.

Feel the satisfaction of the work you will do in this environment. Reach out and take Jesus' hands in yours. Ask Him to bless this space. Tilt your head down and feel Him touch your head as He gives His blessing. He wants you to lead by creating the business you love.

Look into His eyes and tell Him you are depending on Him to make your business exactly what He wants. Ask Him to help you take the next step to grow into the leader He is calling you to be. Talk with Him as long as you wish and listen to what He wants to tell your heart.

Lie there as long as you wish until you are ready to move. Continue breathing deeply until you want to get up and reflect.

Response Activity

Once you have completed the imagery exercise, use your journal or a piece of paper to reflect on what Jesus revealed to you about your work space. How can having a great work environment energize your leadership capabilities? How does it feel to know Jesus is blessing your business and giving you the skills you need to move forward as a leader? Record the feelings and thoughts you experienced as you sat under the palm tree and created for yourself in your space. Record specific things Jesus revealed to you about leading.

Prayer

Thank You, Father, for this time with Jesus. I know I am called to be a leader in my business and in my life. I ask Your help to see leadership opportunities and for help stepping up to those opportunities. Give me a spirit of boldness as I lead in my business.

Thank You for blessing me, thank You for always being there for me, and thank You for leading me into the next phase of my business. In Jesus' name, amen.

Mind Activity

Principle: **God expects me to be a leader in the marketplace.**

Leadership begins on the inside. It is like a three-tiered fountain from which water bubbles up through the center and fills the first cup—you. As this first cup slowly fills, it begins to glide over the edges to the other parts of the fountain. This is you, overflowing to the other parts of your life. You cannot be the person you want to be, or the leader you are called to be, if you have not first filled yourself with God.

In the Soul Activity, you brainstormed and prayed through words you want to incorporate into your leadership style. I have found, for the most part, they fit into four categories: Heart, Hands, Head, and Habits. Where does your style fit in? Look below for your words (or synonyms) to determine your leadership style.

Heart	Hands	Head	Habits
Charisma	Communication	Courage	Character
Passion	Competence	Discernment	Commitment
Positive	Generosity	Listening	Focus
Attitude	Initiative	Problem-	Security
Relationships	Responsibility	Solving	Self-discipline
Vision	Servanthood	Teachability	

Your goal for this principle is going to answer this question: What do you want people to say about you? To build the credibility you want, you must lead in a way that reflects exactly who you are and how you want to be remembered.

When I look through the four categories, I can say I exhibit qualities in each. But, if I am honest, I sit in the Habits category the most. I want people to say I am committed to serving others, focused on bringing my best to the table, and disciplined in how I attack life.

God expects me to lead others in discovering their unique role in the marketplace. My goal reflects this commitment to Him and to the women I serve.

Write out your Goal.

S

M

A

R

T

Here is an example: So I can lead by example, I will continually find ways to improve my knowledge through reading, seminars, conferences, etc. and share my knowledge with the women I serve when I am with them.

Strength Activity

Principle: **God expects me to be a leader in the marketplace.**

To really know how you want others to see you and how you want to be remembered takes showing up authentically every time you are with them. You can impact how others view you by being consistent in living out your life statement. This is really a personal mission statement for your life and business. Since I want you to have all the parts of your life integrated, it is important to think through all the areas of your life to create this statement.

By writing out your life-statement today, you can live it out tomorrow. This is an activity that will bring many of your leadership goals to life.

Think through the following assessment to help you write your life statement:

What I'd like to do:

What I'd like to be:

Seven roles I have in my life:

   1.
   2.
   3.
   4.
   5.
   6.
   7.

Next to each role, write how you would most like to be described in that role.

Ten things that make me feel complete:

1.
2.
3.
4.
5.
6.
7.
8.
9.
10.

Three things I must do every day to feel fulfilled at work:

1.
2.
3.

What I would do if I never had to work another day in my life:

Strengths other people have commented on about me:

Strengths I see in myself:

Write a rough draft of your Life-Statement:

Look through the statement and ask yourself if you have included each of the following questions. Be specific, and use them to continually review your life-statement.

What timeless, proven principle does this Life-Statement reflect?

Do I feel this Life-Statement represents the best that is within me?

Do I feel good about what my Life-Statement represents?

Does this Life-Statement give me direction, purpose, challenge and motivation?

Do I know the strategies and skills that will help me accomplish the Statement?

What's the first thing I need to do today so I can move where I want to go tomorrow?

Prayer

Lord, I thank You that I am called to be a leader. I pray for Your guidance as I strive to live out Your call on my life. I always want to reflect You in every part of my life. Help me step into this role of leadership in all areas of my life. Father, You have given me exactly what I need to follow You, glorify You, and live for You. Please help me be the leader You want me to be. In Jesus' name, amen.

12

Proverbs 31 Woman: Whole, Holy, and Authentic

Read the biblical account of the Proverbs 31 Woman in Proverbs 31:10-31.

Principle: **I am to be whole, holy, and authentic in the marketplace.**

Woman of Valor

I am ending the book with the Proverbs 31 Woman. I know, you probably rolled your eyes and thought, of course, we had to talk about her. Does she make you feel inadequate and tired? She does for me. But upon further investigation, I discovered some interesting facts that made me do a happy dance.

The last part of the last chapter of Proverbs is an acrostic poem that PRAISES women, not prescribes their duties. It was intended for Jewish men to memorize in PRAISE of the women in their lives: mothers, sisters, daughters, friends, colleagues, and wives.

So, shed the shame that comes with your reading of Proverbs 31. We're done with that.

The Proverbs 31 Woman is an example of valor. Whatever you do in your business and in your home, do it with valor. She is not an example of what you should do; she is an example of how you should do it.

The word in Hebrew is chayil, meaning valor. The word is used 246 times in the Old Testament to refer to the strength of fighting men. Each woman in this book demonstrated this strength in various ways: Puah & Shiphrah with their courage toward Pharaoh, Deborah as a judge, Ruth with her fierce loyalty and work ethic, and Rahab with her bold planning, just to name a few.

You have this strength inside of you, too.

Let's celebrate our strength, ladies! We are each unique with different gifts, talents, abilities, and values. We each possess the exact qualities of the Proverbs 31 Woman by just being who we are.

You are enough. If you get nothing else out of this book— though I hope and pray you do—hear that you are enough. You are a Woman of Valor.

Instances of valor are all over your life. It may be easier to see it in other women, but you too have valor. Think of it as a celebration of accomplishments. Valor shows up when a woman fights cancer, runs a marathon, or finishes her college courses. It also shows up in the little things like gaining a client, preparing for a presentation, or playing with her child. Women need to see HOW they are showing up in valiant ways and rejoice with one another. You need to celebrate!

Some words that describe valor are: noble, courageous, brave, heroic, fearless, and bold. In your everyday dealings with family, friends, and business colleagues, I know you display these qualities.

You are a woman who picks up the phone to deal with difficult situations. You are a woman who tackles tasks that seem large and unbeatable. You are a woman who faces adversity in many situations. And you are a woman who has God on your side; He gives you the valor to do it all.

Heart Activity

Reflection Questions:

How have you displayed valor in your life? Describe one or two times you showed valor.

What accomplishments of yours and others would you like to celebrate with other women?

When have you displayed valor in your work? Describe it.

How have the decisions you've made enhanced the lives of those around you?

Prayer

Dear Lord, You are perfect in every way. I thank You for Your complete love for women and for me. You compare the Proverbs 31 Woman to jewels. Help me see myself in her and realize my worth in Your eyes. I pray for strength to do everything with valor. Lord, I trust You for who You are and know You give me exactly what I need when I need it. Create in me the desire to benefit those

You have placed in my life. Help me always look to You for my worth. In Jesus' name, amen.

Women of Valor

What I noticed the most in studying the Proverbs 31 Woman is she does everything to benefit her sphere of influence. Each decision is to enhance her life and the lives of those in her circle. And it's a common theme throughout our biblical businesswomen study.

I think the Proverbs 31 Woman is in each woman we've met; each woman is a Woman of Valor. So now let's see HOW each woman shows up in the Proverbs 31 poem. You will see yourself too—I just know it.

Eve was designed to be a helpmate. Her sphere of influence was with her husband over her children. Work was given to men and women equally in Genesis one and two. She is the mother of all that is living. She was designed so "her husband can trust her, and she will greatly enrich his life. She brings him good, not harm, all the days of her life" (Proverbs 31:11-12, NLT).

Esther was destined to be in position to help her people. She was the example of charm and beauty and feared the Lord. Her mind was sharp and she entered every dealing with strategy and grace. She shows us, "'There are many virtuous and capable women in the world, but you surpass them all!' Charm is deceptive, and beauty does not last; but a woman who fears the Lord will be greatly praised. Reward her for all she has done. Let her deeds publicly declare her praise" (Proverbs 31:29-31, NLT).

Martha directed her household. Through her friendship with Jesus, she changed from the inside out. God never asked her to change who she was, but changed her in ways that gave her peace and contentment. She never stopped working; she embraced the work of her household and the people she loved. "She is clothed with strength and dignity, and she laughs without fear of the future...She carefully watches everything in her household and suffers nothing from laziness" (Proverbs 31:25, 27, NLT).

The Widow in Debt found healing through work. She was put into a desperate situation by following her husband's lead. She turned to her spiritual leader expecting a miracle, but he put her to work. She followed his instructions, showing she trusted him and God. She experienced a miracle by giving all she had and following instructions. In her everyday activity, she could give gratitude to God for His provision. "Her husband can trust her, and she will greatly enrich his life. She brings him good, not harm, all the days of her life...Her husband is well known at the city gates, where he sits with the other civic leaders...hHer children stand and bless her. Her husband praises her"(Proverbs 31:11-12, 23, 28, NLT).

Lydia followed God and became a believer in Jesus. She is the spiritual mother of many. Her personality infused her business and she dressed the part. She made no apology for doing well in her trade. For her, work and worship were not separate; they were part of who she was and how she showed up in her business. Her gift of generosity also created space for the first church in Europe. "She extends a helping hand to the poor and opens her arms to the needy. She has no fear of winter for her household, for everyone has warm clothes. She makes her own bedspreads. She dresses in fine linen and purple gowns" (Proverbs 31:20-22, NLT).

Priscilla displayed wise and loving counsel to those in her sphere of influence. She mentored many in the faith of Jesus who became leaders in the early church. Her effectiveness in seeing truth gave her confidence in God and in what He had called her to do. "She is clothed with strength and dignity, and she laughs without fear of the future. When she speaks, her words are wise, and she gives instructions with kindness" (Proverbs 31:25-26, NLT).

Puah & Shiphrah saved many from death. They developed a plan to defy Pharaoh's order by instructing their workforce (midwives). They were ready to do what is right no matter the consequences. They feared God more than man. They organized the entire Hebrew nation to save their children, including Moses. "She is like a merchant's ship, bringing her food from afar. She gets up before dawn to prepare breakfast for her household and plan the day's work for her servant girls...She extends a helping hand to the poor and opens her arms to the needy...When she speaks, her words are wise, and she gives instructions with kindness" (Proverbs 31:14-15, 20, 26, NLT).

Rahab received the spiritual gift of faith before she even knew God. Her industrious hands devised a plan to save her family in the face of unsurmountable odds. She received divine instructions while working, and when the time of rescue came, she asked for her family's lives to be saved, too. "She finds wool and flax and busily spins it...She makes belted linen garments and sashes to sell to the merchants...She carefully watches everything in her household and suffers nothing from laziness" (Proverbs 31:13, 24, 27, NLT).

Huldah was designated to be an influence as a teacher. She and her husband were well known as the king's and queen's wardrobe attendants, and this gave her elite access to influential people. Her reputation is known and reflects well on her husband and his position. She never stopped learning, and it was rewarded when the nation of Israel most needed revival. "When she speaks, her words are wise, and she gives instructions with kindness...Her children stand and bless her. Her husband praises her: 'There are many virtuous and capable women in the world, but you surpass them all'" (Proverbs 31:26, 28-29, NLT).

Ruth was devoted to God and to her mother-in-law. She worked hard to keep herself and Naomi alive. Boaz called her a woman of noble character even before she had a household and children because of her industriousness. No work was beneath her; she did what was in front of her to do. She was rewarded for her work. "She is energetic and strong, a hard worker. She makes sure her dealings are profitable; her lamp burns late into the night...she carefully watches everything in her household and suffers nothing from laziness" (Proverbs 31:17-18, 27, NLT).

Deborah trusted God for victory in battle. She never put herself before God, but showed courage to lead with God in charge. She depended on Him for her victory. She led the nation as a prophet and judge with wisdom and excellence. "Her husband can trust her, and she will greatly enrich his life...'There are many virtuous and capable women in the world, but you surpass them all!'...Reward her for all she has done. Let her deeds publicly declare her praise" (Proverbs 31:11, 29, 31, NLT).

Each woman in this book is unique; God called each one for His specific purposes. Notice not all of them had husbands, were mothers, worked outside the home, or had sales businesses. None of them were exactly like the other, yet all were Proverbs 31 Women.

The beginning of the Proverbs 31 poem says a Woman of Valor fears God; all our women had that in common. All were clothed in strength and dignity. All were given super-infused valor to do what God called them to do. All exhibited an aspect of the Proverbs 31 Woman that can be admired and celebrated.

The Proverbs 31 Woman is the ideal, not the reality. She exemplifies all parts of you: physical, mental, moral, and spiritual. This woman is the same as the "Wise Woman" described in the rest of Proverbs. Strive to be a Wise Woman of faith—of valor—as you live out God's calling for your life.

Soul Activity

Begin your Praying in Color activity by writing out Proverbs 31:10-31 in your journal or on a piece of paper. Though I quoted the New Living Translation in this chapter, I also like the Amplified Version because it has great synonyms that suggest ways I can see myself. Leave space between the lines and words to be able to mark and color.

Once you write it out, read it and mark words that stand out or speak to you. Mark them with different colors or shapes. Use the same color or shape for words that are similar. As you re-read the verses, make it personal to you. Add thoughts, impressions, words, and pictures God gives you as you use His Word to discover what He has to say to you about being a woman of valor.

Ask God to show you what it means to display the qualities of the Proverbs 31 Woman you possess. Ask Him to show you how to be a woman of valor in your business. Thank Him for who He is and how He has shown you His calling for your life.

Prayer

Lord, I humbly come before You, thanking You that the Proverbs 31 Woman is me. I thank You for giving me the business I have so it can benefit my life and those in my sphere of influence. You have called me to be a woman of valor. Help me live up to that calling. Remind me to do all things for You and to always be looking to You for my significance. Create in me the mindset to see others the way You do. Help me serve others through my business. I love You, Lord, and I live to serve Your purposes. In Jesus' name, amen.

The Proverbs 31 Woman Guided Imagery

This is a guided imagery exercise. Read it through completely before you begin the activity. Refer to the instructions for creating your environment and the breathing exercise in the front of this book to begin relaxing.

After you have relaxed with the breathing, continue to breathe slowly and imagine this scene:

You push against a large rotating glass and wood door and enter an expansive hall. The floor and walls are a beautiful grey marble. Your eye moves up the two flights of wide sleek stairs and travels up further to the skylight ceiling far above.

You are in an art museum. You have come to roam the halls as you think about your own business and dream big about where God wants to take you. Your cross-body bag is light and contains your journal and favorite pen. It's busy here in the lobby of the museum, so you walk up the stairs quickly to get away from the voices. The stairs are set deep and you feel your muscles strain as you climb to the top.

A long hall wraps around to your right. You turn and walk along the smooth floor. You lean over the edge of the stone rail to see below. It is a long way down and you feel a whoosh of light-headedness. You pull back and walk into the first gallery. It is dark with ominous figures from ancient cultures. You cross into another gallery and the paintings are historical depictions.

You walk quickly through one gallery after another, going further and further into the heart of the museum. You have come today to be inspired. You are thinking about your business and what a God-sized dream looks like for it.

You turn left now and enter a gallery of enormous landscapes. The colors, lights, and shadows splash across the oil canvases. You walk over and sit on the lone wooden bench at the center of the room. Only the security guard is roaming in here. He smiles at you and turns away.

The bench is comfortable and just the right height for your legs. You breathe in a long gentle breath and smell the damp coolness of the air conditioning. The room is bright and the landscapes seem to be in motion.

The beauty of one painting catches your eye. It amazes you that the painter could capture the beauty of the earth and sky so precisely. The details jump out and draw you into the scene. You wonder about the process of imagining the scene and putting it onto the canvas. And how big of a vision does an artist need to paint something so big, so impressive?

You turn and take out your own journal and pen. You draw swirls, wavy lines, and shapes. The pen flows easily along the paper. The movement slows your brain, and you are content to doodle and color. God wants to speak to your heart. Imagine Him sitting next to you on the bench; watching you draw.

It is so quiet in this space. Listen. Listen to what God wants to tell you about His vision for your business. Pull up your legs on the wide bench and sit cross-legged with your journal in your lap. Turn to a clean page in your journal and wait for God.

Lie there as long as you wish until you are ready to move. Continue breathing deeply until you want to get up and reflect.

Response Activity

Once you have completed the imagery exercise, use your journal or a piece of paper to reflect on what God revealed to you about the God-sized dream He has for your business. What is your ultimate dream? How will you work it out in the next year? Three years? Five years? How will you get started today? Record the feelings and thoughts you experienced as you sat and listened to what He had to say to your heart. You are a woman of valor. God will give you exactly what you need to live out the God-sized dream He has given you.

Prayer

Father, I am reminded You gave me the business vision I have in my heart. I thank You for creating me to fulfill this calling. I accept that You have big plans for my life and all I need to do is to trust You. Help me take the next step of obedience as I work toward completing this goal. Keep me close to You, Lord, so I know the right decisions to make as I live out my calling. Thank You for giving me such an awesome vision! I want to live my life serving You by serving others through my business. In Jesus' name, amen.

Mind Activity

Principle: **I am to be whole, holy, and authentic in the market-place.**

I am giving you your SMART goal for this principle: I will recognize myself as a woman of Valor—noble, courageous, brave, heroic, fearless, and bold—by celebrating each day the actions and decisions I make for my business to show up whole, holy, and authentic in my sphere of influence.

Strength Activity

Principle: **I am to be whole, holy, and authentic in the marketplace.**

So you can see just how wonderful and valiant you are, I want you to make a list of 100 Accomplishments. You can break it down into ten at a time over a period of days or sit down in one sitting and write them all.

It takes time for you to think about and list 100. You may want to ask family and friends to help. The best way to start is to think about your present life and the things you have accomplished recently. An accomplishment is a task you completed that, when finished, gave you satisfaction. It can be big or small—it's up to you.

Go back in time and think of your life in sections: as a child, in school, as a teenager, in college, at your first job, etc. Use these time blocks to think through what you were doing in your life at that time and what you accomplished that made you proud.

Once you have your 100 Accomplishments, I want you to celebrate. Find your way to give yourself kudos. Then, create an action plan that will include times to reflect on how you are living out your goal and decide what you will do each time to celebrate.

Prayer

Lord, You are amazing! You have created me amazing, too. Thank You. Help me realize how wonderful I am because You made me that way. Help me speak Your truth into my life about who You have created me to be. I pray for You to fill every aspect of my business and my life. I pray to do BIG things for You as You allow me to serve others through my business. I will give You all the glory, honor, and praise. In Jesus' name, amen.

Conclusion

Have the women in this book inspired you to move ahead in your service to God? I hope so. They have for me. My vision for you was that as you read, journaled, prayed, set goals, planned action-steps, and imagined, God would give you clarity on your calling.

It's no mistake that you are alive now with the expertise, gifts, and experiences you possess. He equipped you to live out the vision He has given you. Your job is to trust Him as you take the next step on this adventure called the Christian life.

My prayer for you remains the same as when we started. I pray you have seen God's unlimited resources and understood which ones He has given you to use. I pray you feel His power at work in your everyday life and it emboldens you to live out loud for Him. I pray God has made a bigger home in your heart and that you trust Him more now with your work than you did before. I pray you have grown strong in your faith as you have learned more about the Father's will for you. I pray God's love has so captured your heart that you are sure of His calling on your life. I pray you will continue to practice the habits you established. I pray you will receive a glimpse into ALL God has for you because His adventure for you is bigger than you can even imagine.

This is just the beginning of the adventure. God has placed this book in your hands so you can learn more about connecting your faith and business, to serve Him more. The next step is what I call your Calling Declaration. This Declaration is a direct reflection of God speaking to your heart. It's the meaning and purpose of your life. It's God's measure of success for you because you are living in His will.

This is my Calling Declaration:

> To equip believers to share their faith
> in bold and creative ways
> to their friends, to their family,
> and in their marketplace.

God is amazing in His timing and positioning of where He wants to take each of us.

Are you ready for even more clarity around your calling? Connect with me to take the next step. Find out where the next Calling Clarity Course or Retreat is being held and join the other women who have joined the movement to connect their faith and business to serve God.

Are you ready to continue trusting God and take the next step in His adventure for your life?

Be filled to overflowing,
Deneen

For more information about courses, retreats, and opportunities to work with Deneen, go to www.GrowFromYourOverflow.com.

Resources

Guided Imagery Recordings:

www.GrowFromYourOverflow.com/(name)
/Eve
/Esther
/Martha
/WidowinDebt
/Lydia
/Priscilla
/PuahandShiphrah
/Rahab
/Huldah
/Ruth
/Deborah
/Proverbs31Woman

Password- CLARIFYyourcalling

Websites:

http://biblehelpsinc.org
http://newlife.id.au
http://unlockingthebible.org
http://www.aboutbibleprophecy.com
http://www.beliefnet.com

http://www.biblearchaeology.org

http://www.biblestudytools.com

http://www.ccel.us

http://www.chabad.org

http://www.crosswalk.com

http://www.jrtalks.com

http://www.patheos.com/blogs

http://www.projectinspired.com

http://www.thesacredcalendar.com

http://www.todayschristianwoman.com

http://www.watton.org

http://www.whatchristianswanttoknow.com

http://www.womeninthebible.net

http://www.womeninthescriptures.com

https://bible.org

https://bible.org

https://bible.org

https://bibleview.org

https://en.wikipedia.org

https://jwa.org

https://rachelheldevans.com/blog/3-things-you-might-not-know-about-proverbs-31

https://www.biblegateway.com

https://www.bibleodyssey.org

https://www.decktowel.com/pages/how-linen-is-made-from-flax-to-fabric

https://www.gotquestions.org

https://www.gty.org

https://www.guideposts.org

https://www.openbible.info

https://www.theologyofwork.org
https://www.workingpreacher.org
www.theopedia.com
www.wordlibrary.co.uk

Books:

The Marketplace Christian by Darren Shearer

Working Women of the Bible by Susan Dimickele

Strengthsfinder 2.0 by Tom Rath

Praying in Color by Sybil MacBeth

New American Standard Bible

English Standard Version Bible

New Living Translation Bible

About the Author

Deneen Troupe-Buitrago, M.Ed., is a Motivational Keynote Speaker & Trainer relieving the guilt from Faith-based Businesswomen by connecting Faith & Business. Her organization is called Grow From Your Overflow, LLC.

She is a Development Strategist that connects you to Professional, Personal, and Spiritual growth opportunities through speaking, workshops, online courses, and one-on-one consulting and coaching.

Some areas of expertise include developing goals, writing action steps and time management as well as personal areas such as developing new habits, procrastination and presentation skills. She weaves everything she does with faith and has created the Calling Clarity Course: exploring how God has equipped you for your success in Faith & Business.

Her background in Education mixed with her experience in Drama gives her a unique speaking style that offers a truly hands-on experience. By connecting all of it to her faith, she has combined all the best parts of her life to give back and serve others.

You can connect with Deneen at online at:

Website: GrowFromYourOverflow.com
Facebook: facebook.com/GrowFromYourOverflow
Instagram: @GrowFromYourOverflow
Blog: GrowFromYourOverflow.com/blog
Email: deneen@GrowFromYourOverflow.com